Praise for Sh

"A serious beach book—part real-life underwater adventure, part cautionary tale on the environment, part practical advice on staying safe in the ocean."
                                                          —*USA Today*

"Benchley is a journalist and conservationist, with a genuine sense of awe for the ocean and its fauna, as well as anxiety over mankind's increasing destruction of it. . . . [An] appeal to humanity to better understand and value the delicate balance of marine ecosystems and their members, dangerous or not."
                                          —*San Francisco Chronicle*

"At once a nail-biter and a water-safety guide."
                                          —*San Antonio Express-News*

"Sharks are plainly exciting. . . . Benchley enjoys writing about these creatures, and we enjoy reading about them and watching them—from as far away as possible, of course."
                                              —*The Orlando Sentinel*

"Nearly 30 years after he scared everybody out of the water with a piece of pop culture hysteria called *Jaws*, Peter Benchley spends most of his time trying to convince people that sharks aren't really monsters, even if they do command a certain respect in their home turf. . . . Benchley tells some harrowing true stories and offers practical advice on swimming safely in the ocean."
                                      —*The Atlanta Journal-Constitution*

PHOTO: SCOTT STALLARD

After graduating from Harvard, PETER BENCHLEY worked as a reporter for *The Washington Post*, then as an editor at *Newsweek* and a speechwriter in the White House. His novel *Jaws* was published in 1974, followed by *The Deep, The Island, The Girl of the Sea of Cortez, Q Clearance, Rummies, Beast,* and *White Shark.* He has written screenplays for three of his novels, and his articles and essays have appeared in such publications as *National Geographic* and *The New York Times.* He has written, narrated, and appeared in dozens of television documentaries. He is a member of the national council of Environmental Defense and is a spokesman for its Oceans Program.

SHARK TROUBLE

SHARK TROUBLE
PETER BENCHLEY

RANDOM HOUSE
TRADE PAPERBACKS
NEW YORK

For Stan Waterman
—*sui generis*

Preface
Aliens in the Sea

Shark attacks are natural news leaders. They meet all the criteria for show-stopping spectacle: blood and guts, horror (ANIMAL SAVAGES HUMAN!), and mystery (INVISIBLE TERROR FROM THE DEEP!), and they are highly videogenic. Even if the camera can't get a shot of shark or victim, it can pan the empty beach and the forbidding ocean, focus on the BEACH CLOSED or DANGER: SHARKS signs, and capture the comments of panicky witnesses.

Shark attacks often dominate the news in the summer, as they did in 2001. Newspapers, magazines, radio and television news, and talk shows kept count of the supposed carnage taking place on the East Coast of the United States. Experts were empaneled to speculate on causes and meanings of this sudden, unprecedented assault on humanity.

Never before, to my knowledge, has so much ink and so much

airtime been devoted to so few events of little national and international consequence. Dr. Samuel Gruber of the University of Miami, one of the world's most respected shark scientists, sent the following statement by e-mail to dozens of his colleagues: "I have never seen anything like it in 35 years in the business of shark biology—the media are completely mesmerized by sharks and unlike most sharks the media seem to be feeding on themselves!"

For, the truth was, the hysteria was not justified by statistics or facts. There were not significantly more shark attacks than usual during the summer of 2001, either in the United States or around the world. Though numbers of reported attacks had increased incrementally all during the twentieth century, thanks to increases in the numbers of people living by the shore and swimming in the water and to vastly improved communications, they had leveled off during the 1990s and stayed relatively constant at around sixty to eighty attacks, worldwide, each year. Those are *reported* attacks, granted, but they're the only measure we have.

Shark attacks continued to occur in the United States, with far less than a tenth the frequency of homicides and fatal accidents in the workplace and less than a thousandth that of motor-vehicle deaths. As for shark-attack *fatalities*, well, they're so rare that they're not even on the scale.

I have a "lunchpail degree" in sharks: knowledge acquired not from books so much as on the job—or, in my case, in the water. I have been fascinated by sharks all my life, and have spent more than three decades studying, diving with, and writing about sharks, making documentary films about them, and being involved in the feature films and television movies made from the novels that grew out of my fascination, including *Jaws*, *The Deep*, and *Beast*.

All my life I've been intrigued by sharks of all species, sizes, and temperaments, and I've swum with sharks all over the world, from Australia to Bermuda, South Africa to San Diego, almost always on purpose but occasionally by accident. I've been threatened but never attacked, bumped and shoved but never bitten, and—many times—frightened out of my flippers.

Over the years, I've learned how to swim, snorkel, and dive safely in the ocean, how to exist—*co*-exist, really—with sharks and the hundreds of other marine animals I've been lucky enough to encounter. Hence this book about sharks and other sea creatures, and understanding how to be in the ocean.

In these pages, I pass along what I've learned not only about sharks and how to minimize the chances of getting in trouble with sharks, but also how to maximize the chances of *seeing* sharks, a privilege that is becoming increasingly infrequent.

Shark attacks on human beings generate a tremendous amount of media coverage, partly because they occur so rarely, but mostly, I think, because people are, and always have been, simultaneously intrigued and terrified by sharks. Sharks come from a wing of the dark castle where our nightmares live—deep water beyond our sight and understanding—and so they stimulate our fears and fantasies and imaginations.

For some of us, the fear is a *safe* fear, what *The New York Times,* in an editorial, called "pleasurable cultural hysteria." It is a fear of something that is unlikely ever to happen to us.

For others, though, for those of us who spend much of our lives in, on, or under the sea, it is a genuine fear, and one to be dealt with through knowledge, experience, and judgment.

Of all the oft-cited shark statistics, one that generates very little media coverage and almost no public interest is the most horrible of all: for every human being killed by a shark, roughly *ten million* sharks are killed by humans, sometimes for their skins and their meat but mostly for their fins, which are rendered into soup that is sold (for as much as a hundred dollars a bowl) all over the world and is regarded as a status symbol by the burgeoning middle class in China and other Asian nations.

Sharks are critical to the maintenance of the balance of nature in the ocean (in ways we know, and also in ways we are still discovering) and for us to wipe them out, either through greed, need, recklessness, or simple ignorance, would be a tragedy—not just a moral or aesthetic one, but an environmental one as well—in dimensions we're just beginning to comprehend.

For all we read and hear about "unprovoked" shark attacks, I've come to believe that there's no such thing. We provoke a shark every time we enter the water where sharks happen to be, for we forget: the ocean is not our territory, it's theirs.

None of us would stroll casually into the Amazon jungle, wearing nothing but a bathing suit and carrying for protection a tube of sun cream and a can of bug spray. We know that the jungle is not our natural habitat; we realize we're intruders in the jungle, and that in the jungle there are creatures that regard us as a threat or as prey, and will use every mechanism nature has given them—sting, bite, poison, whatever—to ward us off or attack us. We know that large predators live in the jungle and that, through ignorance or intent, they might regard us as food.

In short, we accord the jungle the respect it deserves.

Yet many people regard the ocean with nonchalance, innocence grounded in ignorance. We need to recognize that, as terrestrials and mammals, we represent a tiny minority on our planet. Seventy percent of the earth is covered by water, leaving to humans a mere three square miles out of every ten.

Of our planet's biomass (the grand total of all living things), more than 80 percent inhabit the seas and oceans. All of those creatures have to eat, from the tiniest copepod up to the largest carnivorous fish in the world: the great white shark.

And so, when we plunge into the water, we must be aware that *we* are the aliens in the sea; we must heed the signs that a shark could be patrolling nearby—signs such as birds working a school of baitfish just offshore, fishermen in small boats with rods bent double and the surface of the water oily with a slick of chum, and other warning signs I'll describe in these pages.

We need to realize that when we go into the sea, we are entering hostile territory, and we should arm ourselves with basic precautions, recognizing that, in the sea, we are fair game to the predators that live there.

I don't mean for a moment that we should stay out of the sea; rather, we need to prepare ourselves, and our children, to swim safely in it. We have, in fact, no choice, for we cannot survive without healthy seas, and I mean that quite literally: the sea sustains all life on earth, controlling our climate and atmosphere, generating the air we breathe and the water we drink.

Only now are we beginning to realize that we have the power to destroy it. And that, too, I mean quite literally. For centuries, human beings have treated the sea as an infinite resource and a bottomless dump. Now we are learning that the sea, like everything else on the earth, is finite and fragile.

This book is about understanding the sea in all its beauty, mystery, and power. It's about respecting the sea and its creatures, many of which are exotic, complex, and more intriguing than anything ever imagined by the mind of man.

But mostly it's about sharks and my experiences with them. Sharks are perfect predators whose form and function have not changed significantly in more than thirty million years. I'll try to pass on what I've learned about sharks and about keeping safe in the sea, to show you what sharks are like and why they don't want to hurt you or eat you, why they would like nothing better than to be left alone to do what nature has programmed them to do: swim, eat, and make little sharks.

Contents

PART I

1

South Australia, 1974
Swimming with Nightmares

LET'S START WITH A STORY ABOUT SHARKS: DANGEROUS REEF, IN THE
Neptune Islands, 1974.

Blinded by blood, nauseated by the taste of fish guts, whale oil,
and putrid horse flesh, I gripped the aluminum bars of the shark
cage to steady myself against the violent, erratic jolts as the cage
was tossed by the choppy sea. A couple of feet above, the surface
was a prism that scattered rays of gray from the overcast sky;
below, the bottom was a dim plain of sand sparsely covered with
strands of waving grass.

The water was cold, a spill from the chill Southern Ocean that
traversed the bottom of the world, and my core body heat was
dropping; it could no longer warm the seepage penetrating my
neoprene wetsuit. I shivered, and my teeth chattered against the
rubber mouthpiece of my regulator.

Happy now? I thought to myself. *Ten thousand miles you flew, for the privilege of freezing to death in a sea of stinking chum.*

I envisioned the people on the boat above, warmed by sunlight and cups of steaming tea, cozy in their woolen sweaters: my wife, Wendy; the film crew from ABC-TV's *American Sportsman;* the boat crew and their leader, Rodney Fox, the world's most celebrated shark-attack survivor.

I thought of the animal I was there to see: the great white shark, largest of all the carnivorous fish in the sea. Rarely had it been seen under water; rarer still were motion pictures of great whites in the wild.

And I thought of *why* I was bobbing alone in a flimsy cage in the frigid sea: I had written a novel about that shark, and had called it *Jaws,* and when it had unexpectedly become a popular success, a television producer had challenged me to go diving with the monster of my imagination. How could I say no?

Now, though, I wondered how I could have said yes.

Visibility was poor—ten feet? Twenty? It was impossible to gauge because nothing moved against the walls of blue gloom surrounding me. I turned, slowly, trying to see in all directions at once, peering over, under, beside the clouds of blood that billowed vividly against the blue green water.

I had expected to find silence under water, but my breath roared, like wind in a tunnel, as I inhaled through my regulator, and my exhales gurgled noisily, like bubbles being blown through a straw in a drink. Waves slapped against the loose-fitting top hatch of the cage, the welded joints creaked with every torque and twist, and when the rope that tethered the cage to the boat drew taut, there was a thudding, straining noise and the clank of the steel ring scraping against its anchor plate.

Then I saw movement. Something was moving against the blue. Something dark. It was there and gone and there again, not moving laterally, as I'd thought it would, not circling, but coming straight at me, slowly, deliberately, unhurried, emerging from the mist.

I stopped breathing—not intentionally but reflexively, as if by suspending my breath I could suspend all animation—and I heard my pulse hammering in my ears. I wasn't afraid, exactly; I had been afraid, before, on the boat, but by now I had passed through fear into a realm of excitement and something like shocked disbelief.

There it is! Feel the pressure in the water as the body moves through it. The size of it! My God, the size!

The animal kept coming, and now I could see all of it: the pointed snout, the steel gray upper body in stark contrast with the ghostly white undercarriage, the symmetry of the pectoral fins, the awful knife blade of the dorsal fin, the powerful, deliberate back-and-forth of the scythelike tail fin that propelled the enormous body toward me, steadily, inexorably, as if it had no need for speed, for it knew it could not be stopped.

It did not slow, did not hesitate. Its black eyes registered neither interest nor excitement. As it drew within a few feet of me, it opened its mouth and I saw, first, the lower jaw crowded with jagged, needle-pointed teeth, and then—as the upper jaw detached from the skull and dropped downward—the huge, triangular cutting teeth, each side serrated like a saw blade.

The great white's mouth opened wider and wider, until it seemed it would engulf the entire cage, and me within it. Transfixed, I stared into the huge pink-and-white cavern that narrowed into a black hole, the gullet. I could see rows and rows of spare teeth buried in the gum tissue, each tooth a holstered weapon waiting to be summoned forward to replace a tooth lost in battle. Far back on each side of the massive head, gill flaps fluttered open and shut, admitting flickering rays of light.

A millisecond before the mouth would have collided with the cage, the great white bit down, rammed forward by a sudden thrust of its powerful tail. The upper teeth struck first, four inches from my face, scraping noisily—horribly—against the aluminum bars. Then the lower teeth gnashed quickly, as if seeking something solid in which to sink.

I shrank back, stumbling, as if through molasses, until I could cringe in relative safety in a far corner of the cage.

My brain shouted, *You . . . you of all people, ought to know: HUMAN BEINGS DO NOT BELONG IN THE WATER WITH GREAT WHITE SHARKS!*

The shark withdrew, then quickly bit the cage again, and again, and not till the third or fourth bite did I realize that there was something desultory about the attack. It seemed less an assault than an exploration, a testing. A tasting.

Then the shark turned, showing its flank, and by instinct I crept forward and extended my hand between the bars to feel its skin. Hard, it felt, and solid, a torpedo of muscle, sleek and polished like steel. I let my fingers trail along with the movement of the animal. But when I rubbed the other way, against the grain, I felt the legendary sandpaper texture, the harsh abrasiveness of the skin's construction: millions upon millions of minuscule toothlike particles, the dermal denticles.

The shark was moving away, upward; it had found a hunk of quartered horse, probably ten pounds, possibly twenty, dangling in the chum. The shark's mouth opened and—in a split-second mechanical replay of the bite on the cage—it swallowed the chunk of horse whole. Its gullet bulged once as the meat and bone passed through on its way to the gut.

Tantalized now, the shark turned again in search of something more to eat. It bit randomly, gaping and snapping as if hoping that the next bite, or the next, would prove fruitful.

I saw a length of rope drift into its gaping mouth: the lifeline, I realized, the only connection between the cage and the boat.

Drift out again. Don't get caught. Not in the mouth. Please.

The great white's mouth closed and opened, closed and opened; the shark shook its head, trying to rid itself of the rope. But the rope was stuck.

In a fraction of a second, I saw that the rope had snagged between two—perhaps three or four—of the shark's teeth.

At that instant, neurons and synapses in the shark's small, primitive brain must have connected and sent a message of alarm, of entrapment, for suddenly the shark seemed to panic. Instinct commandeered its tremendous strength and great weight—at least a ton, I knew, spread over the animal's fourteen-foot length—and detonated an explosion of frenzied thrashing.

The shark's tail whipped one way and its head the other; its body slammed against the cage, against the boat, between the cage and the boat. I was upside down, then on my side, then bashed against the side of the boat. There was no up and no down for me, only a burst of bubbles amid a cloud of blood and shreds of flesh from the chum and the butchered horse.

What are they doing *up there? Don't they see what's going on down here? Why doesn't somebody* do *something?*

For a second I saw the shark's head and the rope that had disappeared into its mouth—and that's the last thing I remember seeing for a long, long time. For when the shark's tail bashed the cage again, the cage slid down four or five feet and swung into the darkness beneath the boat.

I knew what would happen next; I had heard of it happening once before: the shark's teeth would sever the rope. My survival would depend on precisely where the rope was severed. If the shark found itself free of the cage, it would flee, leaving the cage to drift away and, perhaps, sink. Someone from the boat would get a line to me. Eventually.

But if the rope stayed caught in the shark's mouth, the animal might drag the cage to the bottom, fifty feet away, and beat it to pieces. If I were to have a chance of surviving, I would have to find the rope, grab it, and cut it, all while being tumbled about like dice in a cup.

I reached for the knife in the rubber sheath strapped to my leg.

This isn't really happening. It can't be! I'm just a writer! I write fiction!

It *was* happening, though, and somewhere in the chaos of my beleaguered brain I appreciated the irony.

How many other writers, I wondered, have had the privilege of writing the story that foretells their own grisly demise?

2

2001
The Summer of Hype

AFTER SHARK ATTACKS—GENUINE ATTACKS, NOT THE KIND staged from the safety of cages—had dominated the news in the summer of 2001, I contacted George Burgess, director of the International Shark Attack File at the University of Florida, and requested, early in 2002, the latest figures for 2001.

Worldwide, the number of shark attacks recorded in 2001 was seventy-six, down from eighty-five the year before.

In the United States, fifty-five people were attacked by sharks in 2001, exactly one more than in 2000. As for fatalities, five people in the world died from shark bites in 2001, twelve in 2000.

In sum, then, said Mr. Burgess, "2001 was an average year by U.S. standards, and below average internationally. Most important, serious attacks were way down."

Why, then, the shark hysteria of 2001? Because of a conjunction of disparate factors that came together all at once.

There was, first of all, the intangible but everlasting blend of fear and fascination with which human beings regard sharks. Harvard sociobiologist E. O. Wilson put it this way in a 1985 article in *Discover* magazine titled "In Praise of Sharks":

"We're not just afraid of predators," he wrote, "we're transfixed by them, prone to weave stories and fables and chatter on endlessly about them, because fascination creates preparedness, and preparedness, survival. In a deeply tribal sense, we love our monsters."

That love accounts, I think, for the long life *Jaws* has enjoyed as a movie. Aside from the many and manifest merits of the Steven Spielberg film, the core story apparently touches the deep tribal nerve in a great many people.

Then there was the fact that for the first eight months and ten days of 2001, the United States and the world were in a relatively slow "news cycle." Not much was going on that was newsworthy. The controversial presidential election of 2000 was finally over. The economy was slipping, but slowly, and after the Federal Reserve had cut the prime interest rate several times, even that became old news.

Then, at dusk on July 6, eight-year-old Jesse Arbogast was attacked by a bull shark in shallow water off Pensacola, Florida. The attack was particularly gruesome and sensational. Somehow, his uncle wrestled the seven-foot shark to shore and, with the aid of a park ranger, retrieved Jesse's severed arm from the mouth of the shark and rushed it to a hospital, where it was reattached to Jesse. Miraculously, the boy survived.

After that incident, the antennae of the media and the public were set to receive reports of other shark attacks as soon as they happened. And happen they did—the normal encounters between bathers or surfers and sharks that occur, however infrequently, off beaches from New Jersey to Key West.

Each incident was treated as a new sensation, until, very soon, a trend was spotted, and from the trend grew what was seen as a pattern and, eventually, an epidemic. The world was gripped by shark fever.

The fever took hold with such ferocity because of another factor that has come into play over the past few years: the complete alteration in the way news is disseminated around the world.

With the advent of the Internet, cable television, cellular telephones, and satellites, everything that happens anywhere—everything that is said or rumored to have happened anywhere, anything that might possibly have happened anywhere—is ours for the plucking in raw, unedited, unanalyzed, unverified, and (often) unverifiable form.

We choose our news. We decide what's news. We read and see whatever we want, and decide—each in his or her personal wisdom—what is and isn't true.

And thus, no sooner was Jesse Arbogast removed to the hospital than rumors began to fly through the ether, rumors that answered questions no one had asked, rumors that defamed Jesse's heroic uncle: he had been fishing for sharks; he had had this one on his line for an hour; the water was full of blood and chum; children had gathered round to see the shark as the uncle dragged it into shallow water; the uncle was so distraught that he had tried to commit suicide; the reason he was giving no interviews was that he was in the Federal Witness Protection Program . . . and so on.

Not one of the rumors was true.

On August 14 a school of sharks was sighted close to shore near

St. Petersburg, Florida. No one knew how many sharks there were; first reports—by telephone and e-mail—described them as "a bunch." Soon there were "dozens," then "hundreds." By the time a reporter for the *St. Petersburg Times* was assigned to cover the story, the number of sharks was "in the thousands."

The suspicious reporter chartered a small plane and flew out over the scene. He didn't know what to expect; surely, there would be too many sharks to count, but would they be moving toward the beaches or away? Were they chasing food or hunting for food? Was this mass gathering a breeding event . . . or a killing event?

I spoke to him on the phone after he returned.

"The water was murky," he said, "but I could still count the sharks 'cause it was calm and they were all on or near the surface. There were forty sharks. Exactly forty. Even I could see what they were—blacktips—and they were following a school of baitfish, which happens every day. There were more fishing boats out there than sharks, all intent on killing the 'killers.' It was ridiculous."

By the end of July 2001, shark attacks were being reported almost daily—in Florida, North Carolina, Virginia, all up and down the coast. Most of the "attacks" were, in fact, incidents that, in a normal year, would not have merited coverage beyond the local press. But this was not a normal year. The season had been proclaimed "Summer of the Shark" by *Time* on the cover of its July 30 issue, which reached newsstands and most subscribers on July 23.

Though the actual number of incidents was not abnormal, though there had not, as yet, been a single shark-attack fatality in U.S. waters, it seemed to the public that the times were out of joint and the world (or at least the ocean) had gone askew.

And once the public had accepted that 2001 was a particularly shark-plagued summer, experts—often self-anointed—popped up everywhere to offer theories and explanations.

The supposed reasons given for the nonexistent rise in shark attacks included the following:

- The general, overall decline in fish stocks had left sharks desperate for food; consequently, they were attacking humans. There's no evidence, statistical or otherwise, to support this theory.

- Restrictions imposed, since 1993, by the federal government on shark fishing had created an overabundance of sharks, which were now preying on helpless swimmers. The theory ignores all the accepted evidence of a drastic decline in the numbers of nearly every accessible species of shark.

- By targeting certain species and ignoring others, commercial fishermen had inadvertently encouraged a population explosion among bull sharks, which were the villains in several serious attacks. There is no evidence of an increase in the bull-shark population. For a complex combination of dubious reasons, it is *possible* that bull-shark populations have suffered slightly less than species more highly prized by commercial fishermen, but even that has by no means been proven.

- Shark-feeding enterprises, which abound in Florida, the Bahamas, and elsewhere as tourist attractions, had conditioned sharks to associate the presence of humans with the promise of food. When those sharks encounter people who *don't* feed them—for example, swimmers and surfers—they go after the people instead. Not only is this theory unsupported by reliable data or credible anecdotes, it also sparked a squabble in the summer of 2001 between the few scientists who espoused it and the many who dismissed it.

Of all the stories, theories, analyses, and speculations, however, none summed up the lunacy of the summer so perfectly as the cover headline of the September 4, 2001, issue of the *Weekly World News:* CUBA LAUNCHES SHARK ATTACK ON U.S.!

Inside, on pages 2 and 3, beside photographs of Fidel Castro and an openmouthed great white shark, a banner headline shouted, CASTRO TRAINED KILLER SHARKS TO ATTACK U.S.

Datelined "Miami," the story exposed the monstrous plan:

"A cruel plot by depraved dictator Fidel Castro to spread panic and discourage refugees from fleeing Communist Cuba is responsible for the shocking wave of deadly shark attacks along America's Atlantic and Gulf Coasts."

After considering and rejecting other plans, such as releasing poisonous sea snakes along U.S. bathing beaches, Castro, the story said, "came up with the scheme to breed especially ferocious species of sharks and unleash them on the American public—and on Cuban rafters."

The "shark summer" of 2001, which had begun on July 6 with the attack on Jesse Arbogast, ended on Labor Day weekend with two fatal attacks—the only two of the summer in the United States.

On Saturday, September 1, ten-year-old David Peltier bled to death after being bitten on the leg while surfing in the waters off Virginia Beach. Two days later, on Monday, Sergei Zaloukaev, twenty-seven, was killed by a shark while he and his wife, Natalia, were wading in the surf off Avon, North Carolina. Natalia was bitten, too, and lost a foot, but she survived.

The summer ended. Then came the horror of the World Trade Center disaster of September 11, and shark sightings, shark encounters, and shark attacks disappeared from the news.

3

Sharks
How Little We Know

THERE ARE A GREAT MANY SHARKS, AND A GREAT MANY KINDS of sharks, in the sea, and very few—an infinitesimal, insignificant number—will ever have contact with a human being, let alone bother one . . . let alone *eat* one. As a general rule, being attacked by a shark is not something you should worry about—unless you're a person who worries about being struck by lightning, attacked by Africanized killer bees, or murdered, all of which are more likely to happen to you than a shark attack.

Still, there are actions you can take to reduce the odds even further—besides staying out of the water altogether—and there are even one or two things you can do to protect yourself if, God forbid, you ever *are* set upon by a shark. More about both later.

Each of the following statements about sharks has been printed, reprinted, graven in stone, and guaranteed to be the final, unarguable, absolute truth. Of the three, which one, would you say, is true?

1. Of the 380 species of sharks known to science, fewer than a dozen pose any threat whatever to human beings.
2. Of the more than 400 species of sharks in the world, only 11 have ever been known to attack a human being.
3. Of the 450 species of sharks on record, only 3 qualify as man-eaters.

Don't bother to guess, for it's a trick question. The answer is: none of the above. To begin with, nobody knows for certain how many species of sharks there are. Scientists can't agree on how many different species have been discovered and catalogued. Some sharks go by different names in different countries. Australia's gray nurse shark, for example, bears no resemblance to the nurse sharks of the Atlantic and the Caribbean. In some countries, some subspecies are identified as separate species. Most scientists believe that the Zambezi shark and the Lake Nicaragua shark are both bull sharks; a few disagree. Some experts insist that *Carcharodon megalodon,* the fifty-foot monster that roamed the seas thirty million years ago, is a direct ancestor of today's great white shark; others insist just as vehemently that today's makos are the true descendants of *C. megalodon.*

Another reason for the lack of precision about numbers of sharks is that new sharks—new to man, that is—are still being discovered. In 1976 a behemoth virtually unknown to science, nearly fifteen feet long and weighing three quarters of a ton, was caught accidentally by a U.S. Navy ship off Hawaii. A plankton feeder and possessed of a disproportionately large mouth, it was dubbed megamouth. A dozen other specimens have since turned up, everywhere from Japan to Brazil, and in 1990 one was filmed swimming free, after it had been released from the net that had caught it off California. For all its size and heft, megamouth is slow-moving, curious, and not at all aggressive.

More new species of sharks will probably appear as, little by little, we and our miraculous technology turn our focus toward the sea. At least I hope we will, for our record so far has been nothing short of disgraceful.

We have seen less than 5 percent of our oceans; humans have actually visited less than 5 percent of *that* 5 percent.

As a comparison, a terrestrial equivalent of the way in which we have gone about studying the ocean would be if we dragged a butterfly net behind an airplane over the Grand Canyon at night and, based on what we collected, developed theses, hypotheses, and generalizations about life on earth.

Despite the facts that nearly three quarters of our home planet is covered by seawater (of an average depth of two miles), that there are mountain ranges in the ocean higher than the Himalayas, that there is enough gold suspended in seawater to supply every man, woman, and child on earth with a pound of the stuff, and that the mineral, nutritional, and medicinal resources available in the sea are incalculably valuable, for the past half century we have devoted much of our national treasure to reaching and studying a moon that we know to be barren, while spending, relatively, pennies on exploring the rich body of our own earth. Forty years ago John F. Kennedy was already lamenting that we knew more, even then, about the far side of the moon than we did about the bottom of the sea.

We know, really, almost nothing about the ocean, so it's not surprising that we know so little about sharks.

Until recently, there's been no pressure to learn about sharks, for sharks have never had a constituency among the public. Whales, on the other hand, have an enormous constituency. The save-the-whales movement is more than thirty years old, and dolphins, of course, have long had their own legions of devoted humans. (Remember *Flipper*?)

It's true that whales and dolphins are easy to study and easier still to love. They're mammals. They breathe air. They nurse their young and guard them ferociously. They click and talk to one another. They do tricks. They're smart. We can anthropomorphize them, projecting human characteristics onto them. We give them names, and convince ourselves that they respond to—and even love—people they come to know.

Not sharks. Sharks are hard to study and harder still to love. Because they're fish, not mammals, they don't have to come up for air, so they're difficult to keep track of and impossible to count.

And they do have the unfortunate reputation of occasionally—very, very occasionally—attacking a human being and—even more occasionally—eating one.

It's hard to care deeply for something that might turn on you and eat you.

Traditionally, shark scientists, like scientists in many other disciplines, have been highly educated in the library and the laboratory and under-experienced in the field. But there have been—and are still—a handful of outstanding, dedicated shark scientists who are rich in talent, widely experienced in the field, and who have the admirable capacity to, when faced with a particularly perplexing problem, utter the words: "I don't know."

In the United States, Eugenie Clark, John McCosker, Samuel Gruber, and Peter Klimley are heroes to us shark fanatics. Up-and-coming youngsters like Rocky Strong, with whom I worked in South Africa, are devoting their professional lives to the study of great white sharks. And Barry Bruce, with whom I once spent several hours wallowing around inside the corpse of a gigantic great white, is one of the leading shark experts in South Australia.

Of all the benefits that *Jaws*—as both book and movie—has brought me, none do I value more than the opportunity to do television shows and magazine stories with, and learn from, the scientists, sailors, fishermen, and divers who make the sea their home. The new knowledge we've gained since the mid-1970s has convinced me that while almost all of the great-white-shark behaviors I described in *Jaws* do, in fact, happen in real life, almost none of them happen for the reasons I described.

For example, what I and many others at the time perceived as attacks by great whites on boats were, in fact, explorations and samplings. In 1999, in the waters off Gansbaai, South Africa, I witnessed great-white behavior that would have been unimaginable even a few years ago. Large adult great whites approached our tiny outboard-motorboats and permitted a "shark wrangler" named Andre Hartman to cup his hand over their snouts—a risky business he had first attempted in order to guide a shark away from biting a motor and breaking its teeth—at which they rose out of the water, gaped for several seconds as if hypnotized, then slipped backward, down and away, in what I can only describe as a swoon.

Furthermore, the numerous reports I interpreted as intentional, targeted attacks on human beings were, for the most part, cases of mistaken identity. Sharks had been condemned as man-eaters for millennia, and it would be several more years before that core belief would be effectively challenged.

We knew so little back then, and have learned so much since, that I couldn't possibly write the same story today. I know now that the mythic monster I created was largely a fiction.

I also know now, however, that the genuine animal is just as— if not even more—fascinating.

Most shark behaviors, it turns out, are explainable in logical, natural terms.

Sharks are critically important to the health of the oceans and the balance of nature in the sea. Later I'll go into detail about what I perceive to be the value of sharks and why I believe we should appreciate, respect, and protect them, rather than fear them.

First, though, back to Australia in 1974 . . . my first personal year of living dangerously.

4

South Australia, 1974
Part II

THE JOURNEY FOR *THE AMERICAN SPORTSMAN* HAD NOT BEGUN
in that cage in the home range of the great white sharks: the cold,
dark waters near Dangerous Reef in the Neptune Islands. Rather,
the shooting schedule had been designed, wisely, to introduce me
gradually to diving with sharks in the wild, to accustom me to seeing sharks under water, to let me learn, from swimming in company with some of the less imposing species, that while sharks
are, indeed, powerful and efficient predators, they know that
human beings are not desirable prey. No one—I least of all—
wanted me to be so traumatized that I'd refuse to participate in
the "money shots," the moments of peril with great white sharks
in South Australia that viewers would tune in to see. The archives
of *The American Sportsman* contained instances of celebrities
freezing at critical junctures and refusing to go on, sometimes

fabricating elaborate excuses that included sudden summonses to meetings with Hollywood moguls, summonses that had mysteriously made their way to points on the globe so remote as to be unreachable by phone, wires, or radio. (There were no faxes back then, no cell phones, no satellite dishes, no pagers.)

We began on the Great Barrier Reef, where there was no danger of encountering a great white shark because great whites—called "white pointers" by Australians, "white-death sharks" by the tabloid press, "whitey" by the few divers who had been in the water with them—didn't exist on the Barrier Reef. The water there was too warm; white sharks preferred the cool seas of South Australia (and California, New York, and Massachusetts). Also, the Barrier Reef was well charted, well known, and visited year-round by thousands of divers. The ports along the east coast were populated by knowledgeable mariners who could choose specific parts of the reef to dive in, depending on what the clients wanted to see.

The Great Barrier Reef is one of our planet's largest living organisms, an interconnected complex of creatures fifteen hundred miles long. It's the longest, the biggest, the richest reef system in the world, home to the most numbers of the most species of the most beautiful . . . well, you get the idea: it is a living superlative. It has wild areas, savage areas, restricted areas, populated areas, tourist areas, and conservation areas.

It was decided that I should be initiated into diving with sharks by beginning with what Australians call bronze whalers, relatively small sharks (five to seven feet) that tend to gather in schools and are generally regarded as controllable by people experienced in dealing with them, although they can be dangerous when their territory is threatened or when they're fighting over food.

On our first morning on the reef, Stan Waterman had assembled the underwater housing for his 16-millimeter movie camera and—careful professional that he is—decided to take the empty housing into the water, to make sure it retained its watertight integrity—that is, that it wouldn't spring a leak and flood his camera with salt water.

He strapped on a scuba tank, and I, eager to accumulate as much experience as possible under conditions guaranteed safe (so I had been assured), imitated and followed him. We sat on the swim step at the back of the boat—the gaudy reef and sandy bottom were clearly visible through no more than thirty feet of gin-clear water—rinsed our masks, and rolled forward into the sea.

The first couple of seconds of every dive are discombobulating. Surrounded by bubbles escaping from your regulator and your equipment, you're blind and deaf; up feels like down, down like up. Very quickly, though, your eyes adjust, your inner ear orients you in this new space, and you hear the comforting sound of air being inhaled and exhaled through your regulator.

Senses regained, Stan and I nodded to each other and started down.

He saw it first and recognized it immediately; I might have seen it, too, I don't remember, but I certainly didn't know what it was: the pointed snout, the blue gray upper body and stark white underbelly, the perfect triangle of pectoral fins and dorsal fin and—one of the dead giveaways I would soon learn to recognize—the apparently toothless upper jaw, lip rolled under, concealing the rows of sheathed daggers.

It was angling up toward us, slowly, as if idly curious.

Stan touched my arm and looked into my eyes, and there was something so earnest in his gaze—the eyes that normally shone and sparkled were as flat as slate—that I knew instantly what he was saying: Stick with me, do what I do, for we are being approached by a Great . . . White . . . Shark.

My first instinct, of course, was to turn and flee, but by now the shark was within ten or fifteen feet of us, and even in my terror I knew that flight would send a one-word message to the animal: food. So I followed Stan.

Holding his camera housing before him, Stan swam slowly down, directly at the shark. I could see that this was not, in fact, a big white shark, though part of my brain registered it as the size of a rhinoceros. It was about ten feet long, a young male, probably still adapting to the variables in his life, such as water temperature, hunting grounds, feeding methods, and now analyzing prey.

I found myself wondering what we looked like to the shark. Large, loud, bubbling creatures, possibly reminiscent of seals or sea lions in our black wetsuits but substantially different: unafraid (after all, we weren't running but were actually approaching), possibly even aggressive. Still, nothing to be feared; the only things this animal would fear would be larger versions of itself and killer whales.

Silently, we descended; even more silently, it ascended.

Are you crazy? Why are you playing "chicken" with a great white shark?

When we were no more than five feet apart, the shark blinked. Without seeming to flick its tail or alter the pitch of its fins or move a muscle, it changed its arc from up to down and passed beneath us. We stopped and turned, and watched the shark disappear into the gray canyons of the deeper reef.

Once safe back aboard the boat, I protested. "I thought . . . you said . . . you promised . . ."

"I know," Stan said with a grin. "Amazing, isn't it? Can you believe the luck? And I didn't even have my camera!"

"But what about—"

"The first law of sharks," he said, "is this: forget all the laws about sharks."

For the next nine days we waited and watched and baited and dove—day and night, hour after hour—and we saw no sharks of any species or description. We set out chum slicks of fish guts and oil; the crew speared fish and we hung the corpses off the stern of the boat; we prepared savory baits and tied them to brain corals and then hid quietly in crannies in the reef until, one by one, we ran out of air and surfaced and put new tanks into our backpacks and descended again to resume our posts.

We swam free, without cages, for back then (a generation ago) most divers considered cages necessary only when dealing with great white sharks or when filming large numbers of big sharks with reputations for aggressiveness.

The water was warmer than eighty degrees, and our wetsuits kept us comfortable for a long time, but eventually the hardiest of us chilled and began to shiver and, again one by one, we surrendered to the cold and surfaced for good.

With one day to go in this first half of our schedule, we had no film, not a single frame, of any shark in the water, with or without people. Now began the litany of woe from the experts. No one could *imagine* where the sharks could possibly have gone. Bronze whalers were *always* around this area. Why, man and boy, the local crew, had been here, all told, for more than fifty years, and *never* had they seen anything like this. If only we'd been here two weeks ago, the sharks were jumping everywhere. And so on— every excuse ever uttered by every fishing guide and boat captain who has ever struck a dry hole in the ocean.

Our tenth and last day began exactly like the others: clear, hot, flat calm, no breeze, and very little current. The corpse of a big stingray was secured to a brain coral as bait. I dove down and took my position in the sand, kneeling (as instructed) exactly thirty-one inches from the stingray—the optimum distance for Stan's lens to capture, in the same frame, me and any shark that might show up.

After about an hour I had emptied my tank of compressed air, so I surfaced, stretched, warmed myself in the sun for a few minutes, changed tanks, and descended again to resume my station.

Almost weightless, rocked gently by what current there was, snug and cozy in my rubber suit, immersed in the warm, soothing amniotic ocean, I think I fell asleep. I must have, for I have no memory of time passing or of seeing or hearing anything, until I felt Stan tap my shoulder and I opened my eyes and saw, less than an arm's length away, a shark the size of a school bus about to assault our stingray bait.

It was a tiger shark—no mistaking the stripes on its flanks, the peculiar catfishlike protrusions from its nasal passages, the broad, flat head, and the curved, serrated teeth identical in top and bottom jaws—one of the few species of shark that had well earned and long held the title man-eater. Its mouth was open, and the upper jaw had dropped down and rolled its teeth into what is known as bite position.

The so-called nictitating membrane, a defense mechanism in

many sharks designed to cover the eyeball and protect it from the claws or teeth of struggling prey, had slid up and over all but a tiny slit of the yellowish eye—a sign that the shark had decided to bite—had, in fact, begun to bite. It looked, I thought, like a maniac.

Startled as much as afraid, I must have flinched backward, for I felt Stan's hand pushing me forward.

Thirty-one inches, I thought. *That thing is thirty-one inches from my face. My shirts have thirty-six-inch sleeves!* (Yes, I know—so what? But in moments of shock my brain often blows a circuit.)

The tiger shark grabbed the stingray and began to shake it. The huge body (thirteen feet, minimum, was the estimate later) writhed, stirring up a cloud of sand and generating pressure waves that rocked me backward. Conscious of the needs of Stan's lens, I looked for something to hold on to to steady myself, but the only solid structure within reach was the brain coral to which the ray was tied, and I thought that to put my hands *into* the shark's mouth might be . . . inadvisable.

The shark's teeth sawed off one wing of the stingray, then, swallowing, it swam away, swinging in a slow circle to approach the bait again.

As the cloud of sand cleared and settled, movement some-where above made me look up. Halfway to the surface, perhaps fifteen feet away, swimming with agitated movements that pro-jected (to me, anyway) anger and frustration, was a second tiger shark, this one the size of a midsize sedan.

I knew the cause of its apparent distress: in the hierarchy of tiger sharks—and several other species—the biggest feeds first, and this smaller animal, which the consensus would later declare to be about eleven feet long, had no choice but to watch as the tasty hors d'oeuvres were consumed by the larger fellow.

Again the big tiger bit down on the stingray, seeming this time to take in its mouth the entire brain coral, and its teeth tore the carcass to pieces. Shreds of gray black skin flew out through the shark's gill slits and sank to the sand, where tiny fish, brave enough to sortie out into the tumult, snatched them up and retreated to eat them in the shelter of the reef.

I was transfixed, paralyzed not from fear but from fascination and concentration. And then—

Oh, Jesus.

I couldn't breathe. Trying to inhale was like sucking on an empty Coke bottle. Quickly I looked at my air gauge: zero.

I was out of air.

For once I didn't panic, and counterintuitive though it felt, I didn't shoot for the surface. I knew the risk of an air embolism: ascend too fast, holding your breath, and the air in your lungs will expand and blow a hole in a lung, letting slip an air bubble that can travel to heart or brain and kill or maim you. If I was to attempt a free ascent, I wanted to do it properly: drop my weights, open my mouth, and exhale constantly as I swam for the surface.

But I also knew that there was, in fact, at least one more breath of air in the tank, though I'd have to ascend to get it: air that has compressed as a diver descends expands when he ascends, and unless you have truly sucked a vacuum into your tank, chances are there's a bit of crucial, life-sustaining air left.

Of course, to be on the surface above one feeding tiger shark and one tiger shark pissed off because it couldn't feed was not an ideal situation. Still, it struck me as preferable to drowning.

Besides, I didn't intend to stay on the surface for long. I looked up and saw the boat above me. If I angled my ascent properly, I should be able to surface near—if not exactly at—the dive step at the stern.

I turned to Stan and made the "out-of-air" signal—a finger drawn across the throat—then rose off the sand bottom, slowly, as inconspicuously as possible, straightening my legs for the first time in more than an hour and starting to kick.

Both legs cramped, simultaneously and in exactly the same way: my hamstrings sprang taut, snapping each leg up under my body, rendering useless legs, feet, and fins. The sudden pain made me gasp . . . except there was no air to gasp.

Now you are in trouble . . . what to do, what to do, what to do?

I pulled the release on my weight belt; twenty-five pounds of lead dropped off my waist, so immediately I began to rise.

A breath of air became available, and I gulped it down, careful to leave my mouth open to let my exhalation escape.

The last thing I saw before my head popped through the surface was the second tiger shark, swimming in circles beneath me. Alerted by the commotion of my ascent, it had ambled over to see what was going on, and it swam, body tilted slightly, so that I could see its eye watching me.

No worries, mate, I thought. *Just put an arm out and let 'em pull you aboard the boat.*

Frightened, disoriented, and addled by excruciating pain in my locked legs, I extended an arm and . . . nothing. Nobody grabbed it.

I spun in place, and . . . *well, no wonder.* The boat was ten yards away and drifting farther. *No! Impossible! The boat was anchored . . . I was the one drifting.* I was caught in a surface current and being swept away.

I raised my arms, hoping to communicate that I was helpless in the water, and somehow that message got through to our director, Scott Ransom, who grabbed a rope, flung himself off the stern of the boat, and swam to me. Together we held on to the rope, and the crew pulled us to the boat.

I never once looked down. If the tiger shark was pursuing us, I didn't want to know.

Thus ended the "easy" leg of the shoot, the training leg, the get-acquainted-with-sharks leg. From here on, I knew, matters would become serious. We were headed south, to Dangerous Reef, where I would climb into a flimsy cage bobbing in a sea of blood and a crew of dedicated experts would do their best to entice a great white shark to approach the cage and attempt to eat me.

Why, I wondered. *Why did I have to write a novel about a shark? Why not a novel about . . . well, I don't know . . . a puppy?*

5

Jaws

I BEGAN TO THINK ABOUT WRITING *JAWS* IN THE EARLY 1970S. I remember phoning my father, Nathaniel, one day in Nantucket, where he lived year-round. He was a novelist, playwright, screenwriter, and author of children's books. By the time of his death in 1981 he had written seventeen novels, of which the best known was a wonderful story called *The Off-Islanders,* which was made into the movie *The Russians Are Coming! The Russians Are Coming!* He also wrote such enduring kids' books as *Sam the Minuteman* and *Red Fox and His Canoe.*

"What would happen," I asked him, "if you cut a body in two? What would float? Any of it?"

"Depends where you cut it," he said. "Cut it above the air sacs, the lower half will float. Cut it below the air sacs, the upper half will float." He paused, then asked, without a flicker of worry or judgment in his voice, "What're you up to?"

"Trying to tell a story about a shark."

"That's some shark."

"Yup," I said. "I don't imagine anything'll come of it, but I figure, why not?"

"Sure. Nothing to lose."

What I was doing, in fact, was making one final attempt to stay alive as a freelance writer. Since 4:00 P.M. on January 20, 1969, when the Secret Service had forcibly ejected me and a dozen bibulous colleagues from my gigantic office in the Executive Office Building in Washington, where I had labored for the previous twenty-two months as the youngest and least-qualified of President Lyndon B. Johnson's speechwriters, I had had no steady employment.

I was scratching out a few days' work each week from subdivisions of the *Newsweek* division of the Washington Post Company, rewriting correspondents' files into stories for newspapers and TV spots for impecunious local stations across the country, and I was writing articles, on anything, for anyone who would pay for them: book reviews, movie reviews, travel pieces for *Holiday* and *Travel & Leisure,* stories on everything from the nouveau chic to the recession economy for *The New York Times Magazine,* and—most lucratively and enjoyably—reports from Nantucket, Bermuda, and New Zealand for *National Geographic* magazine.

I lived at the time with Wendy and our two small children in a tiny house in Pennington, New Jersey, which was—we had determined after weeks of comparison shopping—the least expensive suburb of New York.

I tried to save a couple of days each week for work of my own (a very writerly thing to say, full of promise that from my spare time would spring a *Ulysses* for the 1970s or a seminal exegesis of the Dead Sea Scrolls). The results were, mostly, short stories that didn't sell to *The New Yorker* and film scripts that didn't sell to anyone. Since there was no room to work at home and I couldn't afford a proper office, I rented, for fifty dollars a month, an empty back room in the Pennington Furnace Supply Company. The manufacture and repair of furnaces isn't the quietest of businesses, nor the most conducive to the flowering of the creative imagination, but since the garden of my imagination appeared to be producing only weeds, little seemed to be lost to the music of sledgehammers against sheet metal.

I was very fortunate to have a literary agent. As a favor to my father, one of his agents, a kindly and generous woman named Roberta Pryor, had taken me on when I was sixteen and had— *mirabile dictu*—actually sold a short story of mine when I was twenty. (I received one fan letter, from a woman who pronounced the story the single most execrable piece of rubbish she had ever read.) In my early twenties I had written a nonfiction book about a journey around the world, and it had sold out its only edition: five thousand copies, I recall, most of which I'm certain were bought by my grandmother. Still, my freelance income was hardly enough to reimburse the agency for postage spent on my behalf.

Roberta refused to give up on me and encouraged me to have lunch with editors from publishing houses, a ritual that provided countless writers with vitally necessary meals and encouragement and, now and then, even generated a viable book idea.

I kept two arrows in my quiver expressly for those lunches. One was a nonfiction idea about pirates—as in, a history of. Pirates had always interested me. The other idea was for a fictional story about a great white shark that lays siege to a resort community. Folded in my wallet was a yellowed 1964 clipping from the New York *Daily News* that reported the capture of a 4,550-pound great white shark off Long Island. I would brandish it at the first hint of disbelief that such an animal could exist, let alone that it might attack boats and eat people.

I believe implicitly, though without a shred of evidence, that every male child on earth is, at some period in his life, fascinated—enraptured! enthralled!—by sharks or dinosaurs or both. Most of us outgrow our obsession. A few—we happy few, we band of brothers—are able to indulge it throughout our lives. I spent my summers, from 1949 to 1961 and occasionally beyond, on the island of Nantucket, whose waters were well populated by sharks: sand sharks, blue sharks, and, once in a great while, a mako. I fished frequently, and on hot and windless oil-calm days the Atlantic Ocean surrounding Nantucket sprouted shark fins like asparagus spears. To me they spoke of the unknown, the mysterious, of menace, prehistory, and adventure—and (when I'd get carried away) of primeval evil.

I had read most of the accessible literature about sharks— there wasn't much—and had seen *Blue Water, White Death*, the 1971 feature film that, for me, remains the finest documentary ever made about sharks. So I knew as much as any civilian about sharks, and I could spin my idea into a yarn sufficient to justify the lunch tab.

Editors went away interested and armed with a vague pledge from me to write an outline—sometime, about something to do with sharks—and I went away and didn't write the outline.

Then, one midday, I had lunch with Tom Congdon, an editor at Doubleday, and when he returned to his office he had the temerity to violate all the rules of the ritual: he called Roberta and offered to pay me money—one thousand dollars—for the first four chapters of an untitled shark novel, to be applied against an overall advance of seventy-five hundred dollars, which would be paid when—and, most critically, *if*—I delivered a complete and acceptable manuscript.

Of course, I fell headfirst into the trap. A thousand dollars was exactly a thousand dollars more than I had at the time; it was nearly half a year's tuition at our children's school; it was . . . well, hell, thirty years ago a thousand dollars was real money.

I signed the paper, took the money, cashed the check, didn't write the four chapters until Roberta told me I'd have to either write them or return the money (which, naturally, had vanished). Then I *did* write the four chapters, and Tom didn't like them because I had tried to write them *funny*. (A funny thriller about a shark eating people is, I soon realized, a nearly perfect oxymoron.) I rewrote the pages, and Tom liked them, so I continued with the rest of the story, which didn't proceed anywhere near as easily as I'm making it appear, but which did, at last, get done, after more than a year of writing and rewriting.

There were problems with the jacket design of the book. One version was rejected by Doubleday salesmen, who said they couldn't sell a book that looked so disgusting: it brought to mind, they claimed, the Freudian nightmare of the *vagina dentata*. Another was too boring. Another was black. Then Doubleday's artistic genius, Alex Gotfryd, found the perfect combination of erotic symbolism (Freudian, but nobody said so), blatant (but acceptable) sexuality, and horror.

There was a problem with the title: we didn't have one. Half an hour before the book was to go into production, there was still no title. Tom and I sat over lunch at a steakhouse called the Dallas Cowboy and reviewed some of the more than a hundred titles we had tried. I had come up with titles reminiscent of French novels in vogue at the time, like *A Stillness in the Water* and *The Silence of Death*. There were monster titles: *Leviathan, Leviathan Rising, The Jaws of Leviathan*. There was *White Death* and *The Jaws of Death* and *Summer of the Shark*. My father contributed *Wha's That Noshin' on My Laig?* and (for the hard-core crowd) *Cunna Linga Here No Longa.*

Finally, when we had finished lunch and Tom had paid the check, I said, "Look, there's no way we're gonna agree on a title. There's only one *word* we agree on, so let's make that the title. Let's call it *Jaws.*"

Tom thought for a moment, then agreed. "At least it's short."

I called my father and told him the title.

"What's it mean?" he asked.

"I have no idea," I said. "But at least it's short."

I called Roberta and told her the title. "That's terrible," she said. "What's it mean?"

"Beats me," I replied. "But it sure is short."

Though no one liked it much, no one had a better idea, so no one disagreed. After all, they reasoned, what we have here is a first novel, and nobody reads first novels, anyway. Besides, it's a first novel about a *fish*, for God's sake, and who cares? At least it's done.

Furthermore—and as a final dose of reality—we all loudly agreed that there wasn't a chance that anybody would ever make a movie out of the book. I knew it was impossible to catch and train a great white shark, and everybody else knew that Hollywood's special-effects technology was nowhere near sophisticated enough to make a credible model of a great white shark.

So we called it *Jaws,* and put it to bed, and that, for the time being, was that.

The book was published in the spring of 1974, to generally favorable reviews. Though the reviewer for *Time* dismissed it, the *Newsweek* critic liked it well enough. *The Washington Post* loved it, and Christopher Lehmann-Haupt of *The New York Times* liked it a lot, but with reservations. I thought that the last line of his review—"Read 'Jaws,' by all means read it, and see if you agree"— was a great "money" line and should be plastered all over every ad (with the minor deletion of the few useless words "and see if you agree"), but Doubleday hesitated to mutilate a quote from a *Times* review.

Nor would they use in their ad campaign my all-time favorite review. Fidel Castro, in an interview with Frank Mankiewicz for National Public Radio, pronounced *Tiburon* (*Jaws* in its Spanish editions) not merely a popular fiction but (I'm paraphrasing here) a marvelous metaphor about the corruption of capitalism. Other reviews declared the book to be an allegory about Watergate and a classic story of male bonding, which Doubleday also declined to publicize.

Jaws was not, in hardcover, the gargantuan best-seller that legend has made it. It climbed slowly up the best-seller list of *The New York Times Book Review,* and though it lingered on the list for forty-four weeks, it never made it to number one. An obstinate book about a rabbit, *Watership Down,* refused to relinquish the number one slot and relegated *Jaws* to months at the bridesmaid's position.

Nor did it sell anywhere near the number of hardcover copies that a comparable best-seller would today. Nowadays, a novel by Stephen King, Tom Clancy, Michael Crichton, or Danielle Steele may sell as many as two million hardcover copies, cover-priced at around twenty-five dollars.

Jaws, priced at $6.95 in hardcover, sold something in the neighborhood of 125,000 copies. If you think that I, as the author, should be able to offer numbers more precise than "in the neighborhood," you're right, but unpredictable returns, multiple editions, and so forth make it difficult to do so.

The story in paperback was entirely different. Sales figures were, if anything, underestimated. It was number one for months on lists all over the world. In the United States alone it sold more than nine million copies. But that success had to do, in part, with the release of the movie, with brilliant cross-promotion by the paperback publisher and the movie company, and with phenomenal good luck.

Film rights to *Jaws* had been bought, for $150,000, by Universal Pictures on behalf of Richard Zanuck and David Brown, two of the few true gentlemen in the movie business. Thoughtful, generous, and honest, Messrs. Zanuck and Brown are widely known for two qualities rare in Hollywood: they don't lie, and they do return phone calls. They permitted me to write a couple of the early drafts of the screenplay, and—knowing that in the heart of many writers lives a secret ham—they actually cast me in the film.

The movie went into production not long after the book was published, which provided additional publicity momentum. I visited the set, played the role of the TV reporter on the beach on the Fourth of July, was cast by the press as being in constant conflict with Steven Spielberg—which was not true but which, through repeated telling, nearly became self-fulfilling—and tried, meanwhile and unsuccessfully, to live a normal life.

Sometime during that hectic spring and summer of 1974, John Wilcox, producer of ABC's venerable television show *The American Sportsman*, contacted me through an old friend to ask if I'd be interested in traveling to Australia to do a show about going into the water (in a cage, of course) with great white sharks. *Sportsman*, which ran for twenty years, from 1966 to 1986, was among the first and best of the "magazine-format" sports shows. Each week it ran three or four segments that featured celebrities from one field participating, as rank amateurs, in one or another outdoor sport. A movie actor might go bass fishing; a baseball player might try bird shooting; John Denver would observe polar bears in the wild (and exclaim, time and time again, "Far out!"), and old chums with legions of nostalgic fans, like Bing Crosby and Phil Harris, would perform duets and exchange light banter while fly fishing and reminiscing by a campfire.

Thus far, Wilcox hadn't produced any scuba-diving segments because there hadn't been any demand for them. Where was the excitement or entertainment in taking a movie camera under water, where the celebrity couldn't talk, and filming fish swimming around on a reef?

Jaws and the tumult attendant on it led Wilcox to believe that sharks—unseen, malevolent, and, best of all, man-eaters—could produce . . . oh, well, the pun is unavoidable . . . monster ratings.

I was a certified diver, though by no means a confidently experienced one. Years earlier, while earning my certification in the

Bahamas, I had seen a shark in the distance, minding its own business, and my reaction had been commonplace: panic. I grabbed my instructor by the arm, pointed at the meandering shark, gestured that it was time for us to surface, and when he calmly refused, breathed so deeply and so rapidly that I sucked my tank dry.

So I agreed to journey to Australia for ABC, on one condition: that I could bring with me one of the handful of people who had ever been in the water with white sharks: Stan Waterman, a cameraman and associate producer on *Blue Water, White Death,* a pioneer in scuba diving who was often referred to as "America's Cousteau," and most important, a neighbor and close friend whom I would trust with my life.

It sounded like fun. After spending the last year and a half locked up in a room alone, writing, it would be a welcome relief, an adventure, a unique experience to recount to my grandchildren, with suitable embellishments, of course.

As with the writing and publishing of *Jaws* and the writing, shooting, and release of the subsequent movie—and, in fact, as with most of the rest of my life to that point—I hadn't the faintest idea what I was about to get myself into.

6

South Australia, 1974
Part III

WE FLEW TO ADELAIDE, SOUTH AUSTRALIA, AND FROM THERE across Spencer Gulf to Port Lincoln, a rugged frontier town in a neighborhood rife with optimistic place-names like Coffin Bay and—our destination—Dangerous Reef.

This was the world of the great white shark and the home of Rodney Fox. Fox had become a national hero in Australia, introducing the *Blue Water, White Death* crew to the great whites of South Australia and embarking on a career as a shark expert, tour guide, and conservationist. Even back then, Rodney knew ten times more than anyone else, scientist or civilian, about great whites, and he was the only individual in the known world who had any notion of how to attract them and film them, under water, in relative safety.

It was Rodney who had built the cages, he who had chartered

the boats and hired the crews and bought the dead horse to use as bait and minced the chum and convinced me that I would be perfectly safe in the cage that was now being hammered to rubble by two thousand–plus pounds of maddened, panicked, and, seemingly, enraged great white shark.

It was Rodney's name that I invoked in vain as I was slammed about in the cage, envisioning myself reduced from a suddenly successful writer to a surf-'n'-turf snack for a prehistoric monster.

The curious thing was not merely that I wasn't afraid but that I *knew* I wasn't afraid. In all the turmoil, the violence, the confusion, the darkness—the sensory overload—my brain made room for a conscious observation about itself. We had departed the realm of fear, my brain and I, and emerged into a peaceful pocket of detached observation. I felt no pain, save for the odd ache accompanying the *thunk* of my insulated bones against the bars. I watched my stubby rubber fingers plucking futilely at the little rubber ring that held the knife in its sheath. Every movement looked slow and deliberate, as if the "play" mechanism in my mental VCR had been slowed to "frame advance."

The noise was raucous, each sound distinct and surprising: the hollow, metallic *whang* of the cage slamming against the hull of the boat; the subdued *whoosh* as a ton of shark flesh lashed wildly through the water; the bubbles blasting both from me and from the rippling gill slits of the huge frightened animal; and, so far in the distance that they might have been imaginary or the relics of a resurrected dream, shrill shards of human voices.

Even my own survival had become a matter more of interest than of anxiety.

The cage began to move, scraping along the bottom of the

boat, and now there was light enough for me to see that we—the shark, the cage, and I—were somehow still connected to the boat above. With a thrust of its tail, the giant body lunged upward and forward.

What's this? Now it wants to board the boat?

Suddenly, with swiftness and grace and in complete silence, the shark slid backward and down, turned, and swam away. The rope had disappeared from its mouth. I had a final glimpse of its tail, and then the shark was gone, absorbed into the misty blue fabric of the sea.

The cage righted itself, but because one of its floating tanks had been punctured, it hung askew. Someone above pulled on the rope, and I felt myself moving up toward the light. Through the moving glassy plane of the surface I saw faces, grotesquely distorted, staring down at me from the boat and, a bull's-eye in their center, the round black eye of the ABC Sports camera lens.

Once on board, I described my ordeal for the camera, nearly weeping with relief.

Rodney, who had undergone (forget merely *seen*) circumstances infinitely worse, enthused with complimentary expostulations like, "You're mad!"

Stan, gifted with a silver tongue, an affection for eighteenth-century diction, and an infinite capacity for ironic flattery, said, "Tell me, sir, is it true that you don't know the very meaning of fear?"

Not till I described what I thought had gone wrong and inquired as to what had, in fact, gone wrong was there an awkward pause. Most of the crew seemed unaware that anything *had* gone wrong, and those few who did know seemed less than eager to discuss the matter.

I chanced then to look up at the flying bridge, where my wife, Wendy, was leaning on the railing and watching with wry amusement the scene below on the stern. We'd been married for ten years by then, and from her expression I knew immediately that she knew everything, from exactly what had gone wrong to who and what had been involved in correcting it. I was confident, too, that whatever had transpired, she had played a role in its satisfactory outcome.

As indeed she had.

In 1974 much of Australia, particularly such outlying states as South Australia, Western Australia, and the Northern Territories, was socially equivalent to Tombstone, Arizona, in the 1880s or Hanover, New Hampshire, in the 1920s. Binge drinking was a national pastime, fistfighting was accepted as entertainment and a valid means of self-expression, and women were regarded as fragile workhorses, delicate termagants, and necessary evils. (A joke of the time asked, "What's Australian foreplay?" The answer: "Brace yourself, Shirley!")

Wendy and I stayed overnight in the Tasman Hotel in Port Lincoln, and when we went downstairs for a drink, we discovered that she was not permitted access to the bar; she could get a drink only in the ladies' lounge.

It was rare, therefore, if not unprecedented, for a wife to accompany her husband on an expedition like ours, living in close quarters on small boats, and Wendy found herself treated with profound awkwardness, though neither resentment nor disrespect.

So when the white shark had appeared and I had climbed into the cage, Wendy was banished from the action, exiled up to the flying bridge.

Admirably, she hadn't argued, and almost immediately she

discovered that she had the best position on the boat, with a comprehensive view of everything that was going on: the giant shark lunging at the baits, bumping and biting the two cages—mine and Stan's—the surface cameraman struggling to keep up with fast-moving figures, ever-changing focal lengths, shifting light, and splashes of blood and oil and water.

She saw the rope attached to my cage slip into the shark's mouth; she saw it catch between the teeth; she saw the shark grow increasingly desperate to rid itself of the cage, thrashing and gnashing and pummeling both cages.

She also saw that nobody else had noticed any of it. They were all too close to the action, too focused on their own tasks. Cameramen were leaning over the transom, trying for close-ups; assistants held on to the cameramen's belts to keep them from tumbling overboard; some crewmen were busy ladling more chum into the water; others could do nothing but stare, openmouthed, as a fish the size of a Buick went berserk behind the boat.

Wendy knew what would happen if the shark couldn't shake loose of the rope, and it became obvious that it couldn't.

She slid quickly down the ladder from the flying bridge, marched aft, shouldered aside one chummer and one idle gaper, and took hold of the rope a foot or two behind the cleat to which it was tied on the stern. She leaned over the stern, trying to see the head of the shark and locate the spot where the rope entered its mouth.

Just then the shark raised its head and lunged upward, and Wendy found herself nose-to-nose with—perhaps twenty-four inches away from—the most notorious, hideous, frightening face in nature. The snout was smeared with red. Bits of flesh clung to its jaws, and rivulets of blood drooled from the sides of its mouth. The upper jaw was down, in bite position, and gnashing as if trying to climb the rope. The eyes, as big as baseballs, were rolled backward in their sockets—great whites do not have nictitating membranes—and as the great body shook, it forced air through its gill slits, making a noise like a grunting pig.

All this Wendy recalled in meticulous detail. She also recalled shaking the rope and yelling at the shark, calling it a son of a bitch and other epithets she wasn't aware she knew, and demanding that it let go of the rope. The shark grunted at her and twisted its head, showing her one of its ghastly black eyeballs, and the rope sprang free.

The shark slid backward off the stern and away from the boat, and when it was fully in the water, it rolled onto its side and, like a fighter plane peeling away from a formation, soared down and away into the darkness.

PART II

7

Six Dangerous Sharks

THERE ARE, I BELIEVE, HALF A DOZEN SPECIES OF SHARKS THAT can, and sometimes do, pose a threat to human beings.

The Great White

First and most notorious is the great white, the shark portrayed in *Jaws*. The largest carnivorous fish in the sea, great whites can grow to more than eighteen feet long and can weigh more than four thousand pounds. They can and sometimes do eat people, though it's now accepted that nearly every attack on a person is a mistake: the shark either confuses the person with a seal or sea lion or, particularly in murky water where it must rely on senses other than its eyes, takes a test bite to determine if this living thing is edible. There *have* been cases of great whites targeting humans, and few though they are, each case generates justified horror.

A few years ago a woman who had been scuba diving near a seal colony was taken from the waters off Tasmania. She had almost gotten to the boat and was reaching out to grab her husband's hand when an enormous great white attacked her from behind and below. While her shocked husband held on to his wife's hand, the shark bit her in half, then returned and took the upper half, literally yanking her torso from her husband's grasp.

Another notorious episode—and one for which no shark expert, scientist, or diver I've spoken with has ever offered a credible explanation—occurred back in 1909. A fifteen-foot-long female great white was caught off the town of Augusta, Sicily, and her belly was found to contain the remains of *three* human beings: two adults and a child.

More than 70 percent of great-white-shark-attack victims survive, because the shark realizes it has attacked in error and doesn't return to finish off the prey. Granted, that figure doesn't take into account swimmers, divers, and snorkelers who simply disappear while swimming in great-white country.

The high rate of survival may have to do with a phenomenon known as the "bite, spit, and wait" thesis of great-white behavior. First advanced by Dr. John McCosker, senior scientist at the California Academy of Sciences, the thesis explains both terminal attacks and attacks aborted after a single bite. According to McCosker, great whites have the astonishing capacity to assess, in the microsecond of a first bite, the caloric value of potential prey. If the shark determines that the prey isn't worth the effort—

that is, won't return as much energy as the shark will expend in attacking and eating it—it breaks off the attack after a single bite. Depending on the ferocity of the bite, the prey may or may not survive.

But if the first bite tells the shark that the prey contains an energy bonanza—as would a nice fat seal, for example, or a sea lion—it will hang around after the first bite, wait for its prey to bleed to death, and then come back to finish the meal.

In general, large great whites perceive human beings as too bony to bother with, so they often depart after that first bite. Of course, when a 2,000- or 3,000-pound fish tastes a 170-pound man, withdrawal can be too little, too late. I will never forget a coroner's postmortem photographs of a young man killed in the Neptune Islands off South Australia. The shark must barely have grazed him before recognizing its mistake, for aside from one deep cut in a thigh and a nasty wound on one hand and wrist, the victim was unharmed. In the photographs he looked as if he was asleep. Sadly, however, the big shark's big teeth had opened two arteries, and the man had bled to death before he could reach the shore.

Some white-shark victims insist that they felt no pain at all when they were attacked, only a *thud* as they were struck and then a feeling of being tugged, as the shark's scalpel-sharp teeth severed flesh and bone. A friend of ours who lost a leg to a white shark while snorkeling off Australia recalled, "I couldn't see it, but I knew exactly what had me. It had me by the leg and was pulling me down. I thought for sure I was going to drown. I've never been so relieved in my life as when I felt my leg let go." Luckily for him, a boat was nearby, someone aboard knew how to tie a tourniquet around his thigh, and he made it to a hospital.

From the swimmer's perspective, the best thing about great whites is that although they exist worldwide, they're extremely rare everywhere. Nature, in its infinite and eternally astonishing wisdom, determined that an apex predator (the absolute top of the food chain) as powerful and devastating as a great white should not exist in vast numbers: the marine food chain couldn't support them. So nature decreed that great whites would breed relatively late in life—not until they're at least twenty years old—and would bear relatively few young, only some of which would survive to adulthood.

Tiger Sharks

Tiger sharks, too, are genuinely dangerous to man. They've been responsible for several attacks off Hawaii in recent years, and it's widely believed, with good reason, that they pose more of a threat to humans than do great whites. Tigers may not be as big or as robust and heavy as great whites, but a fifteen-foot, fifteen-hundred-pound tiger shark is plenty big enough; there are more of them, for they pup many more young than great whites (though some of the rapacious young quickly eat their brethren), and they're ubiquitous. While great whites, as a rule, hang around coastal waters, tiger sharks are completely free-roaming: they're fond of coastal waters, they like to enter lagoons at night and hunt in the shallows for prey that often includes smaller sharks, and they also roam the deep.

Once, when I was on a boat over the abyssal canyons off

Bermuda, a huge tiger shark cruised leisurely around our stern, as if showing off its formidable size. The top of its head was as big around as a manhole cover, and the long, slender striped body seemed to take forever to pass by the stern. It was a chilling sight, reminiscent of the crocodile in *Peter Pan* that waits for Captain Hook to fall overboard. To me, the message from this giant said, *Take your time, no rush, I'm in no hurry, but sometime, someday, one of you will make a mistake and enter my realm, and then you'll be mine.*

Suddenly, though, the shark must have received a signal that real potential prey was nearby, for it sped away and, a few seconds later, exploded through the surface fifteen or twenty feet behind the boat, clutching in its jaws an adult sea turtle. The turtle was too big to swallow, its shell too tough to crack; its head and legs had withdrawn into the safety of the carapace. The shark shook the turtle violently from side to side and then, mysteriously, let it go and slipped silently beneath the surface.

For several moments we watched the turtle bobbing on the surface, head and legs still invisible, and we guessed that the shark had abandoned the effort and departed in search of easier prey. The turtle must have come to the same conclusion, for slowly its legs protruded from the shell, then came the head, and then . . .

Bammo! Like a rocket, the shark blasted up from below, clamped its jaws on one of the turtle's hind legs, and worried it with its teeth until, at last, the leg came off. The remaining three legs and the head snapped back inside the shell; again the shark slid away under water; again the turtle bobbed on the surface.

For the next half hour or so, we saw the assault repeated again and again, though without further success. Once wounded, the turtle appeared to be prepared to hunker down inside its shell forever, if necessary. As much as we rooted for the turtle—we knew it could live a successful life with three functioning legs—there was no way we could interfere; nor did we want to, for this was normal, natural predation in the sea.

Bull Sharks

The third shark that poses a true threat to man in the sea is the bull shark, which comes in several varieties, including the Zambezi shark, the Lake Nicaragua shark, and several of the so-called whalers of Australia. As the first two names imply, bull sharks are even more wide-ranging than tigers; they have been found in—and have killed people in—lakes and rivers. Most sharks can't survive, not to mention hunt and feed, in even brackish water, but bull sharks are equipped with some biological quirk that permits them to function normally in salt, brackish, and *fresh* water.

Bull sharks also frequent shallow water and murky water, like that off the Gulf Coast of Florida. It was a bull shark that attacked young Jesse Arbogast in July 2001, triggering the media frenzy that lasted all summer, and Bahamians asserted that bull sharks were probably the culprits in the two nonfatal attacks a month later in the shallow waters off Grand Bahama Island. Bull sharks have such a bad reputation for being aggressive, fearless, and territorial that they undoubtedly are blamed for more attacks than they're responsible for. Still, there are so many bull sharks in so many waters in which so many people choose to swim that they must be classified as extremely dangerous.

Oceanic Whitetips

Then there's the oceanic whitetip, whose Latin name so aptly describes the creature that I'll burden you with it: *C. longimanus,* or "long-hands." This shark's pectoral fins are extraordinarily long and graceful, resembling the wings of a modern fighter jet. *Longimanus* tends to stay in the deep ocean, and nobody on earth has the vaguest notion about total numbers of long-hand attacks because the people they do attack are either adrift, alone, or survivors of shipwrecks, who don't much care *what* species of shark it is that's harassing them. I'd bet that many of the crewmen of the *Indianapolis,* in 1945, were killed by long-hands, but no one will ever know.

I do know, however, that *longimanus* is unpredictable, scary, and demonstrably capable of killing a human. There's a story about one that attacked two U.S. Navy divers in the deep waters of the Tongue of the Ocean in the Bahamas. The shark took a big bite out of one of the divers and then, as the diver's mate fought it for possession of his friend, dragged the diver into the abyss. Finally, at a depth of about three hundred feet—far beyond safe scuba depth—the mate had to choose between letting go of his friend and dying himself, and he watched as shark and body disappeared into the gloom.

Long-hands are my personal bêtes noires—one of the few species of shark of which I am genuinely and viscerally afraid. A couple of decades ago one made an honest effort to eat me. I don't blame the shark for trying, because my situation fell well within the bounds of Stupid Things You Should Avoid at All Costs, but the near-miss scared me—and scarred me permanently—nevertheless.

I was with an ABC-TV crew, also in the Tongue of the Ocean, in open water more than a mile deep. We had tied our boat to a Navy buoy that had become a popular spot to film because it had been in the water for so long that the sea had claimed it, transforming it into an artificial reef. Microscopic animals had taken shelter in the buoy and the chain and had been followed by tiny crustacea and other small critters. Then the larger ones had come to feed, and those larger still, until—in the magical way the sea has of generating life on all levels—the entire food chain had come to use buoy and chain as a feeding ground.

A school of yellowfin tuna was swarming around the buoy, attracted by something, and in the brilliant sunlight of the summer day the colors were so gorgeous that we decided to take some footage for the film segment about the Bahamas that we were working on for *The American Sportsman*.

I, as the so-called talent, was dispatched into the water. Stan Waterman followed to film whatever happened—presumably nothing more than the contrasting colors of the beautiful fish against the cobalt sea, interrupted now and then by a black-rubber-suited human wearing a yellow "horse-collar" buoyancy-compensator vest around his neck.

Back then I was still a pretty green blue-water diver. Blue-water diving is diving in water with no bottom visible or reachable; it can spark fears and phobias, for to look down into the darkling blue nothingness is to harken back to childhood nightmares about monsters and infinity. I wasn't accustomed to diving in water I knew to be more than five thousand feet deep, and once in a while I was haunted by a vision of my body drifting down, down, down, from light blue to darker blue, to purple and violet and the unknown black.

So, naturally, whenever I had to dive in blue water, I carried a security blanket: a sawed-off broomstick about three feet long, attached to my wrist by a rawhide thong. Exactly what it was supposed to protect me from I never determined, but my logic was unassailable: if cameramen could carry cameras with which to ward off attackers, and assistants could carry cameras and lights, why shouldn't I be allowed to carry a broomstick?

Thus armed, I jumped overboard and swam among the yellowfin tuna—or, rather, they swam around me. I held on to the barnacle-covered buoy chain to keep from being swept away by the current, and the school of tuna, which had scattered when I splashed into the water, re-formed and circled me. The shafts of sunlight piercing the surface glittered on their silver scales and yellow fins, and it seemed to me that Stan must be gathering an entire library of beauty shots.

The water was very clear, visibility more than a hundred feet, I was sure, though it's hard to tell in blue water, for there's nothing visible against which to gauge distances.

At the very edge of my vision I saw a shark swimming by. I couldn't discern what kind it was, and I didn't much care, for it was ambling, really, and showing no interest in me or the tuna.

Meanwhile, far up on the bow of the fifty-five-foot boat, one of the crew—bored and tantalized by the sight of so many delicious meals swimming so close to the boat—rigged a fishing rod, dropped a baited hook into the water, and let it drift back into the school of tuna. He had not asked permission, nor had he told anyone what he was doing, for—hey, who cares?—he was staying out of the way and minding his own business. When he hooked a fish, he would simply drag it up to the bow and haul it aboard, and no one need be the wiser.

Stan gestured for me to move away from the buoy, so that he could frame me and the fish cleanly against the blue background. I let go of the chain and kicked my way out into open water. Obligingly, the tuna followed.

Suddenly I was gone, jerked downward by an irresistible force, with a searing pain in my lower leg, arms flung over my head, broomstick aiming at the surface. I could see Stan and the tuna receding above me. I looked around, panicked and confused, to see what had grabbed me. The shark? Had I been taken by the shark? I saw nothing.

I looked down. I was already in the dark blue; all that lay below were the violet and the black and . . . *wait . . . there, against the darkness . . . what could it possibly—*

A tuna, fleeing for the bottom, struggling, fighting . . . *fighting? Against WHAT?*

Then I saw the line, and the silvery leader. The fish was *hooked*, for God's sake. Somehow it had gotten . . . *no, impossible, no way it could have—*

A cloud billowed around my face, black as ink, thick as . . . blood. *My blood.*

I leaned backward and kicked forward, wanting to see my feet.

The steel leader was wrapped around my ankle. The wire had bitten deep, and a plume of black was rising from the wound, a sign that I was already down very, very deep, for blood doesn't become black till the twilight depths. (The sea consumes the visible spectrum of light, one color at a time, beginning a few feet under water. Red disappears first, then orange, yellow, green, and so on, until, when you reach 150 or 200 feet, blood looks black.)

All I could guess was that, in some implausible fluke, as the fish had fled the surface it must have passed between my legs, or circled around my feet, or *somehow* wrapped the leader around my leg. And all I knew was that, somehow, I'd better find a way to free my leg before I was taken to depths from which no traveler returns.

I reached for my knife, to cut the line, but—encumbered by gear and disoriented by fear—first I couldn't find the knife, and then I couldn't release it.

The tuna stopped diving and turned, and the change in pressure against its mouth, the release of resistance, must have convinced it that it was free, for it swam upward, toward me.

The line slackened, the leader eased and spread, and I slid my foot and fin out through the widening coil.

Giddy with relief, I checked my air and depth gauges: 185 feet deep, 500 pounds of air, more than enough for a controlled ascent but nowhere near enough for a decompression stop, if one was necessary, a contingency about which I knew nothing. Diving computers were still years in the future (as were any computers for the common man). Because I hadn't intended to leave the surface, certainly not to venture deeper than, say, ten feet, I hadn't consulted the standard of the day: the U.S. Navy's decompression tables, a reliable guide—though calibrated for a twenty-five-year-old male in peak physical condition—to safe diving at various depths.

How long have I been at this depth? At any depth? How long have I been in the water? No idea.

I started up, slowly, and now the black blood no longer billowed around me but trailed behind. The pain in my leg had waned, and my foot seemed to be working, which meant that no major tendon had been cut.

I passed a hundred feet, then ninety, eighty . . . things were lighter now, visibility had returned, and I could see the rays of the sun angling down from the shimmering surface. Everything would be okay, after all. There was noth—

The shark came straight for me, emerging quickly from the blue haze, its fins forming a triangle of lopsided symmetry because of the slight downward curve of the extraordinary pectorals.

Ten, maybe fifteen feet from me it veered away, banked downward, and passed through the trail of blood leaking from my ankle. Convinced now of the source of the savory scent it had picked up from far away, it rose again, leveled off before me, and began the final, almost ritual, stage of the hunt.

Because seawater acts as a refractive lens, sizes are difficult to ascertain under water. The generally accepted rule is that animals appear to be roughly a third again as large as they actually are. This shark looked ten or twelve feet long, which meant that, in fact, it was probably seven to nine feet long. But "in fact" didn't matter to me; all I cared about was that the closer this shark came, the bigger it looked, and near to me or far, it was very big.

It circled me twice, perhaps twenty feet away, establishing for itself a pattern and perimeter of comfort, and then began gradually to close the distance between us. With each circle, it shrank the perimeter by six inches, then by twelve, then fifteen.

I raised my broomstick and held it out like a sword, waving its blunt tip back and forth to impress upon the shark that I was a living being armed with the weapons and determination to defend myself.

Longimanus was not impressed. It circled closer, staying just beyond the reach of the broomstick. I could count the tiny black dots on its snout, the celebrated ampullae of Lorenzini, which carry untold megabytes of information, chemical and electromagnetic, to the shark's control center.

The mouth hung open about an inch, enough to give me a glimpse of the teeth in the lower jaw.

As I turned with the shark, trying to maintain some upward movement, I watched the eye—always the eye—for movement of the nictitating membrane, the signal that the threat display was ending and the attack itself beginning.

It quickened its pace, circling me faster than I could turn, so I began to kick backward as well as upward, to increase the distance between us.

I jabbed randomly with the broomstick, never touching flesh, never causing *longimanus* even to flinch.

I glanced upward and saw the bottom of the boat, a squat, gray black shape perhaps fifty feet away, forty-five, forty . . .

The shark appeared from behind me, a pectoral fin nearly touching my shoulder. The mouth opened, the membrane flickered upward, covering most of the eye, the upper jaw dropped down and forward, and the head turned toward me.

I remember seeing the tail sweep once, propelling *longimanus* forward.

I remember bending backward to avoid the gaping mouth.

I remember the ghostly, yellowish white eyeball, and I remember stabbing at it with the broomstick.

I *don't* remember hitting, instead, the roof of the shark's mouth, but that's what must have happened, for the next thing I knew, the shark bit down on the broomstick, shook its head back and forth to tear it loose, and, when that failed, lunged with its powerful tail, intent on fleeing with its prize.

The broomstick, of course, was attached to my wrist, and I was suddenly dragged through the water like a rag doll, flopping helplessly behind the (by now) frightened shark, which had taken a test bite from a strange, bleeding prey and now found itself dragging a great rubber *thing* through the water.

Breathing became difficult; I was running out of air.

I tried to peel the rawhide thong off my wrist, but the tension on it was too great and I couldn't budge it.

I was on my back now, upside down, my right arm over my head as *longimanus* towed me away from the safety of the boat. I could once again see blood trailing from my leg; at this depth it was dark blue, and it streamed behind me like a wake.

Everything stopped. At once. My arm was free, and I was floating, neutrally buoyant, about thirty feet beneath the surface. I looked at the broomstick—or at what remained of it: *longimanus* had bitten through it, and the strands of mashed wood fiber looked splayed, like a flowering weed.

Far away, at the outer limits of my sight, I saw the black scythe of a tail fin vanish into the blue.

I sucked one final breath from my tank, opened my mouth, tipped my head back, and propelled by a couple of kicks, ascended to the kingdom of light and air.

Not until I reached the swim step at the stern of the boat did the weakness of fear overcome me, and the shock.

I spat out my mouthpiece, took off my mask, and gurgled something like, "Goddamn . . . son of a *bitch*! . . . mother—"

"No!" said the director. "No, no, no. You can't use that language on network television. Go back down and surface again and tell us what you saw."

Makos and Blue Sharks

The final two sharks on my personal list of species to be wary of could not be more different from each other. One, the mako, is a loner that reminds me of Jack Palance in *Shane:* sleek, silent, and vicious. The other, the blue shark, is a pack animal that rarely bothers anyone but has, on occasion, killed human beings floating in the ocean. Because it is a pelagic (open-water) shark like *longimanus,* the blue shark is vulnerable to large commercial fishing operations, and over the last ten years populations of blues all over the world have been devastated.

The mako is one of the fastest fish in the sea—far and away the fastest shark—and is the only shark listed by the International Game Fishing Association as a true "sport fish." The feel of most sharks on a fishing line has been likened to hauling on wet laundry or trying to lift a cow; fighting a mako has been compared to riding a bull or wrestling a pissed-off crocodile.

Makos leap completely out of the water, turn somersaults, and "run" in any and all directions in their frenzy to escape. Hooked makos have been known to charge boats and jump *into* open cockpits, where they've gone berserk and destroyed the boat that has hooked them. (A mako, remember, can weigh upward of a thousand pounds.) Some fishermen have jumped overboard rather than risk being beaten to death by the flailing fish, and a few have tried to subdue maddened makos by shooting at them with high-powered rifles—a technique not recommended, because of possible unintended consequences.

While the body of a mako is one of the most beautiful in the sea, its face is positively ugly. A mako *looks* mean. Its teeth, upper and lower, are long, pointed, sharp as needles, and snaggly. Unlike a great white's teeth, which speak to me of quick, efficient death, a mako's teeth warn of a nasty end, of flesh ripped into ragged chunks. A mako's eye, too, is distinct from every other shark's. To me, at least, it looks crazed and threatening, like a coiled snake, ready at any second to explode into unstoppable violence.

A mako's speed, however, is its most dazzling weapon. Especially over short distances—like the range of visibility in most water conditions—it is capable of appearing and disappearing as if by magic: a gray ghost in the distance one second, right in front of you the next, gone the next, back again the next.

A friend of mine was snorkeling in shallow water in the Bahamas a few years ago, poking the sand bottom with a long metal rod in search of buried cannons or shipwreck wood, when he glanced up and noticed a shark cruising at the far limit of his vision. Here's what he recalls:

"I didn't give it a thought, didn't pay any mind to what kind it was. Before my eyes had refocused on the bottom, it hit me. Out of nowhere. I never saw it coming. All I knew was, I felt like I'd been hit by a freight train. My mask was knocked off, both flippers came off, I dropped the spear, and suddenly the water was full of blood. Mine. The mako had hit me just once, a glancing blow, tore up my thigh pretty badly. I could see him off a ways, hanging there, like he was deciding whether or not I was worth eating. Then—*poof!*—he was gone. I guess he figured I was too bony."

Bony, perhaps; lucky, definitely.

Any Shark Can Ruin Your Day

Don't take as gospel my (or anybody's) list of bad actors in the company of sharks. All such lists are subjective. Mine includes only sharks that either I or my colleagues have had trouble with. Some folks, for instance, have reason to be scared of hammer-heads; others have had unhappy run-ins with gray reef sharks.

What you *should* take as gospel—and what subjective lists ignore—is the most important fundamental precept of dealing with sharks, that is, *any* shark *can* be dangerous. Still, most injuries inflicted by reputedly inoffensive sharks are caused by human error or ignorance.

Nurse sharks, for example, are among the most docile of all species. The common peril people face from them is being bumped by them as they flee. I know of at least one diver, however, who, when he entered a cave and saw a nurse shark sleeping in the sand, pulled the shark's tail to get it to move. The shark moved, all right; startled awake, it spun around in a frantic blur, bit the man in the throat (missing an artery by a couple of millimeters), tore a gold chain from his neck, and, as it fled the cave, knocked the man spinning against the rock wall.

Over a single August weekend in 2001, in the single Florida county of Volusia, six people were bitten by sharks *that they saw before they entered the water*. The sharks (most were blacktips) had gathered to feed on schools of baitfish; the people had gathered to participate in a surfing contest. Too impatient to wait for the sharks to finish feeding and leave the area, the surfers chose instead to wade among and step over the feeding sharks.

That only six were bitten seems to me a miracle.

Other attacks last year happened to people who ignored, or were ignorant of, one or more of the basic rules that help keep the chances of an attack to a minimum: they swam at dawn or at dusk; they swam alone; they swam far from shore or where fish were feeding or birds were working.

Elsewhere in the world, a man was almost killed when he tried to hitch a ride on the back of a whale shark, as harmless a giant as ever roamed the sea. When he grabbed the enormous dorsal fin, his hand slipped, then *he* slipped, and hung in the water, watching, as the great speckled body moved beneath him like a ship. Mesmerized, he forgot that this ship was driven not by a propeller but by a tail as tall as he was and as hard as iron, and the sweeping tail clubbed him from behind, rendering him breathless and senseless. He survived only because an alert buddy located his regulator mouthpiece, rammed it into his mouth and purged it—forcing air into him—and inflated his vest, which lifted him to the surface.

There is one circumstance under which all sharks of all sizes and (nearly) all dietary predilections will eat a human being without hesitation. That is if the person is dead.

Sharks are scavengers. Scouring and clearing the ocean of animals that are weak, weary, or dead is one of a shark's most valuable functions.

8

Swimming Safely in the Sea

AT APPROXIMATELY NINE O'CLOCK ON THE MORNING OF JULY 23, 2001, four young cousins—three girls and a boy, aged eleven to sixteen—waded into knee-deep water at a beach in Far Rockaway, Queens, New York.

Although lifeguards assigned to the beach were not scheduled to begin their shift for another hour, the youngsters were accompanied by an adult, an uncle, who was reportedly aware of the dangerous currents off this particular stretch of beach. He warned the children not to go into the water while he busied himself preparing fishing rods and fetching food for their picnic.

The children probably thought they were obeying; wading wasn't really going into the water.

Within minutes, three of them were dead.

While the uncle's attention was elsewhere, all four had been yanked off their feet by the waves, and grabbed and dragged under water by a current so violent that it had already earned the area its local nickname—"the death trap." Only one of the children, the eleven-year-old boy, managed somehow to escape the grip of the current and get back to shore.

The next day's newspapers were replete with warnings against swimming on unguarded beaches, and official warnings about the price the public pays for ignoring regulations.

The pertinent issue, however—the real reason those three girls and more than four thousand other people in the United States drowned in 2001—has nothing to do with rules, regulations, or lifeguards.

It has to do with the public's unfamiliarity with the ocean and ignorance about swimming safely in it.

According to the American Red Cross, more than 54 percent of Americans—perhaps as many as 140 million people—say that their primary leisure activity is swimming. That's more than all our golfers, tennis players, sailors, scuba divers, and Frisbee artists combined. Off the record, though, those same Red Cross officials acknowledge that only about 12 percent of the professed swimmers are actually competent swimmers.

And God only knows what tiny fraction of that 12 percent are competent *ocean* swimmers, a specialty that takes as much knowledge, training, and experience as rock climbing or kayaking. A Red Cross–certified beginning swimmer is about as close to a skilled ocean swimmer as a licensed driver is to an Indianapolis 500 contestant.

The United States has 12,383 miles of shoreline, of which much less than 1 percent is patrolled by lifeguards on any given day. So if, on a hot summer day, you're struck by a sudden urge to swim in the sea, the odds are that there won't be a lifeguard nearby to keep an eye on you.

I began to swim in the ocean at the age of five, shepherded diligently by an uncle who had been disqualified from serving in the armed forces during World War II because of a bad back. Swimming in the sea was his passion and his therapy, and because there were no lifeguards on most of the beaches on Nantucket, he wanted me to know how to take care of myself.

He taught me how to study the water before I went in, how to enter the water without getting bashed by a wave, how to select the wave appropriate for me to ride, how to ride it and recover from the inevitable mistakes I was bound to make. He taught me that swimming in the ocean meant working *with* the ocean, never against it.

My uncle's first, indelible lesson, writ large, was: *Never fight the ocean. Go with it and it will work with you. Let it take you where it will, and it will let you go.*

It's the most important single dictum in ocean swimming. If everyone who swam in the ocean obeyed it, the number of drownings would shrink dramatically.

People who get into trouble in the ocean are prone to panic. If the past is any guide, somewhere between twenty and forty people *a day* will drown during the summer in the United States, most of them within fifteen feet of safety, and all because of panic.

If you are a young, healthy, sober person, there is no reason for you to drown while swimming in the ocean if, before you go into the water, you learn the basic facts about the environment into which you're about to go, learn how to coexist with it and cope with its caprices. Some people harbor the belief that they can out-muscle the ocean. No one can. And yet there are some who will die trying.

Here are some basic lessons I've learned and some simple precautions to take that will help keep you and your children from getting into trouble while swimming off a beach. They require nothing more than a rudimentary knowledge of how oceans work, the patience to study the water you're about to enter, and a healthy dollop of common sense.

Ocean Water Is Always Moving

It's a fact you must take on faith: no matter how calm the surface may appear, the water beneath is never still. It is moving in three dimensions: back and forth along the shore, in and out from the beach, and up and down to a degree dependent on the slope of the shelf of the beach.

Water is driven constantly by wind, tides, and currents, and by local phenomena like channels, jetties, and points of land. The presence (or absence) of reefs, shoals, and sandbars will alter water's motion; prevailing winds will drive surf onto certain beaches and leave others to be lapped by little but the tides.

If you intend to swim in the ocean on a given day, it makes sense to stand for a moment and study what the water is doing that day. The wind will be pushing waves onto the beach, and since winds rarely blow directly *at* a beach, the waves will strike the shore at an angle, causing a current called a "set" or a "drift" that moves the water in a particular direction.

Look at swimmers already in the water or at pieces of wood or seaweed floating on the surface, and note which way they're moving and how fast. That will tell you how strong the drift is and how quickly you'll be carried away from the point where you enter the water. The stronger the drift, the closer you should stay to shore and the more carefully you should plan where you want to exit the water, because here is another inexorable fact of ocean swimming:

You Cannot Swim Against a Strong Current

If you try, you will exhaust yourself and probably precipitate a chain of events that may lead to disaster: fatigue, gasping, breathing water, choking, panic, struggling for air, waving or calling for help, sinking, and, finally, drowning.

If you want to emerge from the water near your blanket, your Yoo-hoo, and your can of Pringles, walk up the beach in the opposite direction of the drift, enter the water, and let yourself float down the beach until you reach your exit point. Then swim gently *across* the drift toward shore. Otherwise, be prepared to float away from your home base and walk back when you're finished swimming.

Under *no* circumstances should you try to swim against the current—the only exception being for swimmers with a lot of experience in the ocean and a dedication to vigorous exercise. For years I swam a mile a day for exercise, and when I was at the shore, I'd calculate the drift with the intent of swimming as hard as I could against it while managing to stay in place. I was always alert, though, for the onset of fatigue, and when I saw myself slipping away from a fixed point on the shore, I'd immediately swim across the drift and get out of the water.

There are a few naturally occurring phenomena that can sometimes (but not always) be seen from the shore, that can be deadly but don't have to be, and that you can anticipate—just by being aware of them—whether or not you see them coming.

Undertow

This is a term that is universally known and widely misunderstood. Many people use *undertow* to mean *any* action of waves, currents, or tides that can jeopardize their safety. In fact, undertow is a very specific phenomenon that occurs mostly on narrow beaches with steep scarps, or drop-offs. It is, simply, the action of water thrown ashore by a wave returning whence it came.

After a wave breaks, gravity will carry the water back to sea. If the drop-off into the sea is steep, the water will fall sharply, carrying you with it. If you don't struggle or resist, the undertow will carry you for a few feet (perhaps more, but not much more) and will then dissipate. Buoyed by the air in your lungs, you will rise to the surface, and you can swim back to shore. You may find yourself in water over your head, but if you're not comfortable being in water deeper than you are tall, you are, in the purest sense of the phrase, out of your depth.

Runout or Sea Puss

A common cause of multiple simultaneous problems is known both as a "runout" and a "sea puss." Somewhere offshore of a relatively straight beach there will be an invisible sandbar or shoal that has built up over a long period. Untold millions of tons of water will flow over the bar toward shore, until, at last, the level of the water inside the bar exceeds the water level outside the bar, at which moment, inevitably, the water must begin to flow back seaward.

If there is a weak spot in the sandbar, it may collapse and create a funnel-like path through the bar. The enormous volume of water—which always seeks the easiest path to equilibrium—will rush toward the funnel with unimaginable power and irresistible force.

Runouts happen frequently, and they can be seen from the beach. People watching one have described the scene as like seeing the entire ocean running down a drain. A strip of water leading out to sea, perhaps ten yards wide, perhaps fifty, will look different from the rest of the ocean. It will definitely have its own motion; it may contain short, choppy, foamy waves; the water will look murky and sandy from turbulence; all manner of flotsam— pieces of wood, seaweed, trash—will be speeding seaward in the strip. If there is wave action over the sandbar, the runout will appear as a gap in the surf, for this is where the bar has collapsed. Once beyond the sandbar, the strip will vanish as the water disperses and the runout has . . . well . . . run out.

For veteran surfers, runouts are a blessing, for they provide effortless transport over the bar and beyond the waves. Surfers know that if at any point they change their minds, they can return to calm water simply by paddling across the runout until they're out of it.

Swimmers caught in runouts have that option, too, but most either don't know it or, in shock and surprise, forget it. They panic and, intuitively, try to resist the force of the runout instead of, counterintuitively, surrendering to it and, when they're ready, swimming across and out of it.

Swimmers have another option, too, but it takes a cool head and a practiced eye to choose it. If a swimmer caught in a runout can see the sandbar offshore (or the waves breaking on it) and can determine that it isn't too far to swim safely back from, she can—no kidding—relax and enjoy the ride. The runout will carry the swimmer past the bar and, perhaps twenty or twenty-five yards farther out, will dissipate, leaving her to return to shore—maybe even pleasantly, by riding one or more of the waves that break over the bar.

That second option may be a bit more of a challenge than the average swimmer wants to assume, but once more, if you're not fit enough to swim, kick, float, or dog-paddle for a couple of hundred yards in the ocean, don't go in.

Undertows and runouts are phenomena that affect only swimmers, for they occur *in* the water, or, in the case of runouts, offshore. You can't be caught in one if you don't go swimming. That's not quite the statement-of-the-obvious that it appears, for there *is* one ocean imp that can reach up onto the beach and grab you (or, especially, your small child) and drag you into deep water. An old Environmental Science Services pamphlet called it a "killer at the seashore." Its common name is a "rip."

Rip

The reason a rip is so dangerous is that it actually forms *on* the beach. Children wading in the wave wash where a rip begins— like the four in Queens mentioned earlier—can be knocked off their feet and sucked out to sea in a matter of seconds.

Beaches are, by nature, unstable. The mixture of sand, pebbles, rocks, shells, vegetation, and water that makes up a beach is soft and malleable, and its contours change with every wave that passes through and over it. All day long erosion creates small depressions, in random sequence, up and down the beach. Water from returning waves will gravitate toward the depressions, scouring them deeper and wider and creating, very quickly, a strong seaward pull—a rip.

If a child is standing at the edge of such a depression, the ground will suddenly disappear and the child will be sucked away from shore. If the natural slope of the beach is long, gentle, and shallow, the child may be able to struggle out of the rip, sideways, into calm water. But if the slope is short and steep, the child will be in turbulent, deep water before he can catch a breath.

Rips resemble runouts in both appearance and solution. Like a runout, a rip is a strip of rough, murky, foamy water moving directly away from the beach. A rip begins right *at* the beach, however, and it tends to be narrower than a runout, anywhere from a few feet to a few yards wide. It doesn't travel as far—dissipating, usually, just beyond the breakers—and it can end as abruptly and unpredictably as it began, while other ones may be forming at other spots along the same beach.

A swimmer caught in a rip has the same options as a swimmer caught in a runout: swim across the rip until you're out of it, or let it carry you out until its force fades away. Whatever you do, *don't fight it*; don't try to swim straight back to the beach. That way lies exhaustion, panic, and, perhaps, drowning.

To me, one of the saddest aspects of drowning is that it is so often unnecessary, the result of compounding a simple error or two.

Years ago, I wrote a piece for *The New York Times Magazine* on how to swim safely in the ocean, and in it I quoted a description of a typical drowning victim, told to me by a veteran Red Cross safety expert named Mike Howes:

"He [the hypothetical victim] decides he's in trouble, so to attract attention he waves his arms over his head, which puts a lot of meat out of water—where it's heavier—and makes him sink. He struggles up again, gasps for breath, then waves his arms again and sinks again. If he left his arms in the water and waved them slowly up and down, he'd stay on the surface. But he doesn't, so he gets water in his mouth; his epiglottis slams shut, and he panics. He coughs, sinks, coughs under water, gasps, and—well, that's it."

What most swimmers fail to realize is that if they are uninjured and even marginally competent, they can save themselves. In all but the roughest and coldest seas, they can stay afloat indefinitely. They can also, without great effort, propel themselves toward shore. They may end up several miles from where they entered the water, but they'll be alive to gripe about the walk home.

One day in my late teens I was swimming with a friend off the south shore of Nantucket when we found ourselves trapped offshore, beyond the breaking point of endless, tremendous waves. There were no surfboards, body boards, or boogie boards back then—at least not on Nantucket—so all we had for flotation and transportation were our own air-filled lungs and our own strong young arms and legs. We had been riding the waves happily for an hour or so and had paid no attention to where we were in relation to the shore. We weren't aware that we had been swept away from the long, sloping beach where the waves broke in regular, pre-

The most notorious face in nature: a great white shark, upper jaw dropped into
"bite position." In fact, though, this was a moment of curiosity, not aggression.
The shark had poked its head out of the water and was just
having a look around. South Africa, 1999.

A great white shark that circled our tiny boat several times off Gansbaai, South Africa, in 1999. When we boarded the boat, the captain said, "Rule number one: if anybody falls overboard and a shark grabs him, the person next to him jumps down onto the shark's head. That startles 'im and makes 'im let go. Usually."

Nature's perfect creation: a great white shark approaching a bait (*above right*) and eyeballing a diver in a cage (*right*). Essentially unchanged for tens of millions of years, great whites have no enemies except bigger versions of themselves, killer whales, and, of course, man. No one knows for sure how many great whites still exist, but the evidence, anecdotal and scientific, suggests that the magnificent animals are threatened everywhere and, in many parts of the world, actually endangered.

The shark approaches the cage (*above*) and prepares to take a test bite.
After completing a circle of the cage, the shark comes at it from
a different angle (*below*) and lifts its head out of the water to swallow a bait.

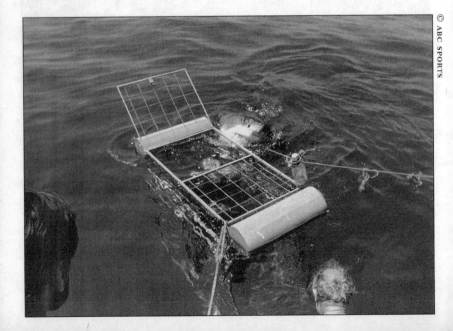

Shark's view of me in the cage (*above*). Do I look appetizing? I don't think so. *Below,* my fantasy becomes reality: the first great white shark I ever saw underwater. South Australia, 1974.

The shark has snagged the tether rope in its teeth. Cowering in the cage, armed only with my trusty broomstick, I alone realize that chaos is about to ensue.

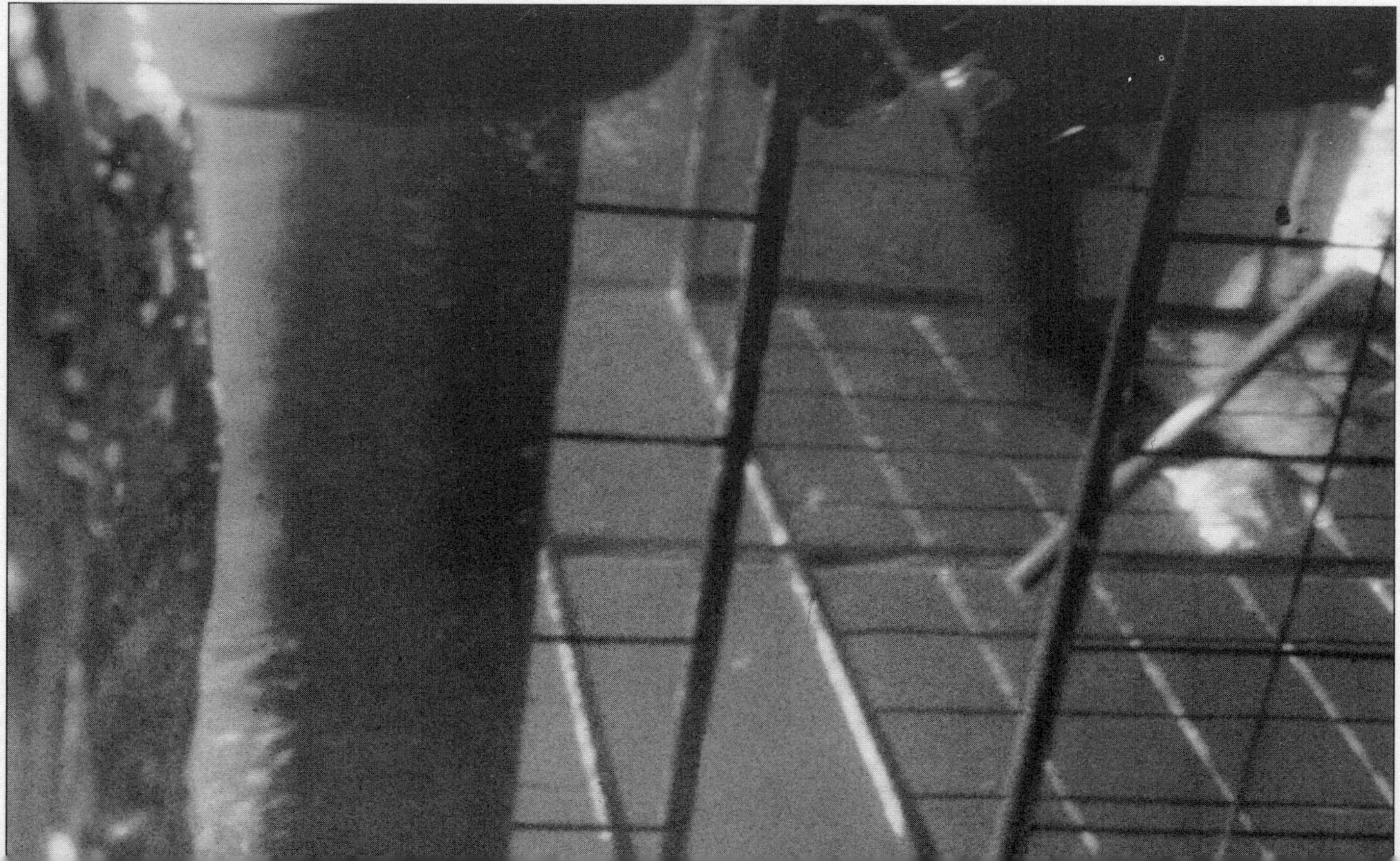

WEEKLY WORLD NEWS

September 4, 2001 — $1.69 U.S. / $1.99 CANADA

Shroud of Turin opens its eyes!

Castro's evil plot to terrorize our beaches!

CUBA LAUNCHES SHARK ATTACK ON U.S.!

3-BREASTED WOMAN, 3-ARMED MAN HAVE 3-LEGGED BABY!

The summer of hype—2001. *Left:* one newspaper's attempt to explain the supposed explosion in shark attacks on humans. *Above:* a completely phony computer-generated image that was circulated on the Internet during the summer. No wonder shark-attack hysteria gripped the nation.

Above: on the beach set of *Jaws* in the cold spring of 1974. Left to right, my wife, Wendy; PB; Roy Scheider (Chief Brody in the movie); and, in front of me, our five-year-old son, Clayton. *Below:* Steven Spielberg preparing me for my scene as the television reporter on the beach on the Fourth of July.

Above: the intrepid reporter interviewing Richard Dreyfuss (Hooper) during the Fourth of July beach scene in *Jaws*. *Below*: on the set of *The Deep* in Bermuda, 1976. Nick Nolte (*left*) had starred in the TV miniseries *Rich Man, Poor Man*, but this was his first leading role in a major feature film. The leather-covered cigarette lighters hanging around our necks, each with the name of the movie, were gifts to cast and crew from the gutsy, game, and gorgeous Jacqueline Bisset (*right*).

Two of the most memorable shows (for me) from ABC's *The American Sportsman*.
Above, as yet unaware that I'm leaking blood from a wound
in my ankle, I've become an object of desire for an oceanic whitetip.
My celebrated broomstick is about to meet its end.
Right, riding a giant manta ray in the Sea of Cortez. A second after he
took this picture, Stan Waterman had his face mask knocked off and
his nose bloodied by one of the manta's wings.

© STAN WATERMAN

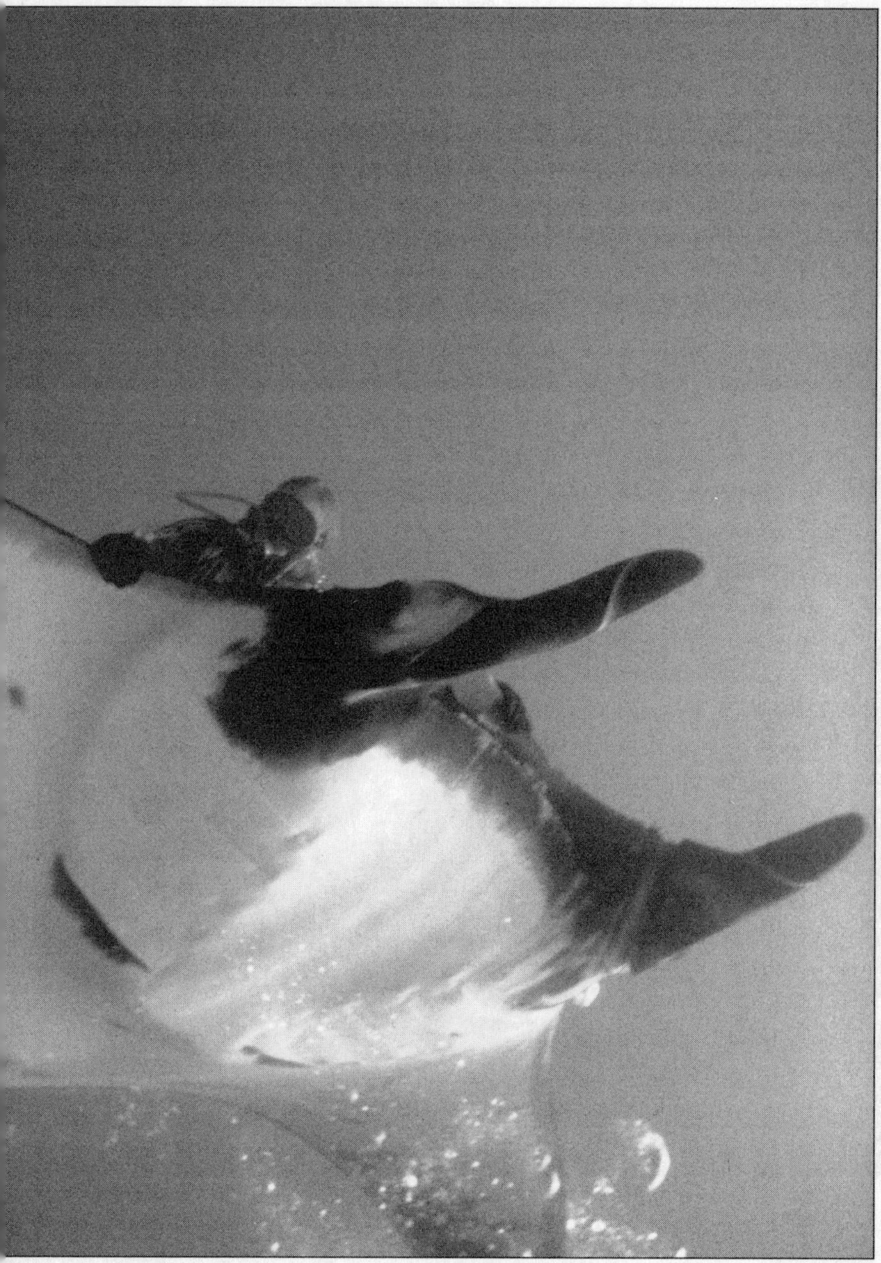

Stan Waterman, *near right*, one of America's pioneer divers and underwater filmmakers, a gentle man of consummate charm and grace. *Below:* Stan greeting— while attempting to film— a whale shark, the biggest fish in the sea.

Above: an armada of scalloped hammerheads in the Sea of Cortez. No one knows for certain why they gather in such numbers—perhaps it's a ritual related to breeding— but they seem to have no interest whatsoever in human beings.
Left: a silvertip in the South Pacific, one of the "sharkiest-looking" of all shark species.
Below: one of several species of bull shark—unpredictable and dangerous.

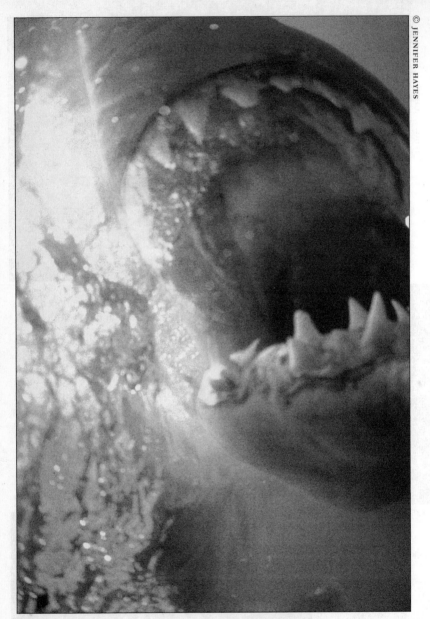

Prey's-eye view of a great white ambushing from behind and below.
Many professional shark wranglers believe that if you're under water and a great
white shows an aggressive interest in you, the smartest thing to do is ascertain
that the shark *knows* you've seen it. Great whites depend so much on the
element of surprise for a successful attack, says this theory, that if they know
you've seen them, more often than not they'll abandon the attack on you
and go instead in search of easier prey.

dictable rhythms and carried us all the way in to knee-deep water. Now, we were surprised to find, we were far offshore of a steep, relatively short beach and a precipitous hidden sandbar that, together, produced row after row of tall, rough waves that crested high and broke almost straight downward.

We would try to ride a wave, but instead of being carried gently ashore, we would be slammed violently onto the hard-sand bottom, "boiled" mercilessly in the sandy foam, and then propelled upward to more or less the same place where we had begun—just in time to duck under another monster wave, and another. After making virtually no progress for, I don't know, ten, fifteen minutes, we were both exhausted. We knew that our only salvation lay *off*shore, in the calm water beyond the waves.

Turning seaward, we swam under breaking wave after breaking wave until, finally, we reached open water where ocean swells had not yet become waves.

We were, we guessed, between a quarter and half a mile offshore. Though from this prospect we couldn't see the waves actually breaking onshore, we could see their massive shoulders gather and hunch before they disappeared, to be instantly followed by the next rank of waves and the next.

We knew very well that there was no way we were going to make it to shore in these conditions. We also knew, though, that we had nothing, really, to worry about. Nantucket was only fourteen miles long; we had entered the water at approximately the midpoint of the island; we were heading westward where, at the end of the island, shallow shoals extended far offshore.

We were cold, yes, because the water temperature was only in the upper seventies, but if we stayed active, we could keep from freezing for many hours. Save for an unimaginable stroke of bad luck—being eaten by something, say, or being run down by a nuclear submarine, the odds against both of which were similarly astronomical—we could float safely indefinitely, or at least until we reached a time of slack tide or a point at which we could walk ashore.

We'd be inconvenienced, surely, and grumpy and tired and cold. We'd be forced to hitch a ride, soaking wet and sandy, back to our car. But we would be alive.

It took four hours, but that's what happened. Along the way, we passed several populated beaches—the people were so far away that they resembled the tiny virtual passengers on the cinematic *Titanic*—even one overseen by a lifeguard, but we raised no alarm, for we didn't want to put anyone's life in jeopardy by asking them to rescue us. Besides, we were fine; we didn't need rescue.

Sometime in midafternoon, we came to a part of the island where the shoals extended so far out to sea that wave action ceased—there was no shelving beach for them to break on—and was replaced by a short, confused chop that we could, at first, swim through and then, at last, wade through.

We were everything I described above, plus chastened and grateful. I said a silent "thank-you" to the uncle of my childhood.

Drownproofing: A Survival Technique

Everyone who would swim in the sea should be compelled to learn an excellent survival technique called "drownproofing," invented in the 1940s by a swimming coach named Fred Lanoue. Endorsed by the U.S. Public Health Service and taught at many schools, it's easy to learn and, as much as anything can be, idiot-proof. (It is not, however, panicproof. Nothing is.)

The two premises of drownproofing are: (1) most people will float if their lungs are filled with air; and (2) it's much easier and less tiring to float vertically than horizontally. Most people's bodies *want* to float vertically, buoyed by the two big air sacs (the lungs) that stay near the surface, and with the heavy (bony and muscular) hips and legs dangling beneath.

Here's how to drownproof yourself:

Floating vertically, with your hands limp at your sides, take a deep breath, hold it, and let yourself hang there, with your face in the water and (optional but more relaxing) your eyes closed.

As soon as you feel that you'd like to take a breath—long before that awful feeling when you know you *must*—exhale slowly through your nose. Raise your arms, and cross them in front of your face. Spread them as if you were parting curtains, and when your arms are extended, push your palms down toward your sides and tilt your head back. Your mouth will come out of the water. Take a breath, lower your head and arms, and let yourself bob in the water.

Every movement should be easy, deliberate, unhurried. You're not trying to go anywhere; there's no rush and no worry. When you hear your pulse—and you will, for the rhythms of your body become the focus of your mind—it should sound normal, not rapid. Fear and excitement waste energy and oxygen.

I can hear you muttering, "Easy for *you* to say." But that's why you're practicing, so that if and when the time comes for you to save yourself, you'll be ready.

It won't take you long to feel at ease with the technique of drownproofing. When you do, leisurely lift your head out of the water, flutter-kick gently until your body is horizontal, and then—on your back, with your hands paddling easily at your sides—kick as often as is comfortable in the general direction of the shore.

If you tire, stop kicking, let your legs hang down again, and resume the drownproofing breathing until you feel you're ready to carry on. Remind yourself that you're not trying to "beat" the sea, nor is it trying to beat you.

We humans sometimes have an unfortunate tendency to anthropomorphize not only animals but the sea itself. We use words like *treacherous, savage,* and *killer* to describe natural phenomena like waves, currents, and storms. It is, I think, a symptom of our refusal to admit that we must coexist with nature, not compete with it or attempt to dominate it.

We *are* nature, and nature is us. We are of the sea and from the sea, and if we choose to venture into the sea, we must respect and appreciate it for what it is: an environment that is different but not hostile, accommodating to the educated and prepared, and fatal mostly to the foolhardy.

9

How to Avoid Shark Attack

YOU'VE HEARD AND READ IT A THOUSAND TIMES: THE CHANCES of your being killed by a shark are so tiny as to not be worth worrying about.

The odds against being *attacked* by a shark are nearly as long, but the issue here is as much semantic as statistical. Very, very few encounters between swimmers or snorkelers and sharks result in what could be considered an actual *attack*.

I think of an attack as what a grizzly bear does when she's protecting her cubs, or what wolves, bears, and even rats do when they're cornered or threatened. In general, sharks do not attack people; the exceptions happen mostly to scuba divers who unwittingly venture across an invisible line that a shark considers to be its territorial border and then either don't see, don't understand, or choose to ignore the obvious warnings issued by the shark.

When a shark feels threatened or crowded, or when it senses that its territory is being violated, its posture changes; its back hunches; its pectoral fins drop; sometimes it shakes its head back and forth; always it looks and acts agitated. It is saying—broadcasting, *shouting*—"Get out of here! This is *my* turf." Fish get the message; they scatter and disappear into the reef. People sometimes don't, with the result that the shark attacks: it rushes in, bites, and, usually, retreats to wait and see if the intruder withdraws.

For the most part, what we're talking about when we use the words *shark attack* are really shark *bites,* one step in the shark's normal feeding pattern, motivated not by rage, fear, or frenzy but by curiosity, confusion, and hunger.

Semantics aside, the chances of your being bitten by a shark are ridiculously small. If you added up the shark-bite incidents reported around the world in a given year and divided the total by the number of man-hours spent in the water, you'd get some unfathomable figure like .000003, which would enlighten you not at all.

But if you swim in the sea, there does exist a tiny chance of your being bitten by a shark. The good news is that there are ways to reduce that chance to very close to zero.

Over the past twenty-five years, in the United States and many other countries around the world, there has been a vast shift in population toward the seashore. In the U.S. alone, some 50 percent of our 280 million people now live within fifty miles of the shore. Millions of people who did not grow up near the sea and who know nothing about it are now exposing themselves to the sea, with all its beauty, power, mystery, and danger.

Many are venturing into the sea without according it respect for what it is: the largest environment on the planet, home to more animals than any other—all of which must eat in order to survive. It is an environment in which most of us are not only aliens but also clumsy and ill-equipped to survive.

And yet on every glorious day of every summer, men, women, and children around the world plunge into the sea, taking risks that they shouldn't . . . most involving drowning but some involving creatures that sting, pinch, and bite. Including sharks.

That's why I believe that practically no shark bite is unprovoked. We provoke sharks simply by going into the water, entering their feeding grounds, becoming fair game.

There are some practical steps to take to reduce the risk of shark bite, and the first requires a bit of a change in one's worldview, a shift of focus from the utopian to the real.

These days, most of us are so rarely in danger from anything in nature that we've become complacent. We assume we're safe everywhere. Australians are an exception, because they're brought up to *know* that their lovely nation is home to innumerable dangerous living things. The rest of us have been conditioned to Bambi-ize the animal kingdom, so we tend to regard every animal as warm, cuddly, and friendly, or, sometimes, simply afraid of us. So little are we exposed to wild animals that we have no real knowledge of how to behave around them.

On land, our ignorance is rarely tested: deer eating flowers in the backyard aren't a threat to life and limb. But when we choose to venture into the sea, we can't afford to be complacent. Among the many millions of creatures living there is the world's only large, free-roaming predator that poses a genuine—and sometimes mortal—threat to man in an environment in which he freely chooses to go: the shark.

And sharks can be anywhere: in shallow water or deep, in the surf itself, even, occasionally, profiled against the face of a breaking wave. They can be in the little dips between the shore and sandbars just offshore, where low tide sometimes traps them. They can be in murky water or clear, rough water or calm.

Furthermore, while only a few species of sharks are considered dangerous to man, *all* sharks—especially all sharks over three feet long—should be respected and avoided by swimmers. I've been hassled by a school of three- and four-foot-long sharks, and what began as a game of push-and-shove soon turned into a terrifying mass mugging from which I barely escaped, with bite marks on my fins.

Before you enter the water, stand for a moment and look at the sea around you. If there are birds working offshore—swooping and diving into a school of baitfish on or near the surface—that's a sign that larger predators are underneath, driving the baitfish upward.

Perhaps those predators are bass or bluefish, but perhaps a shark or two could be stalking the bass or bluefish. Any signs that schools of fish—of any size—are in the neighborhood can indicate the presence of sharks. If you see a concentration of ripples on the surface of the water, or silvery flashes as feeding fish roll out of the water and their scales catch the sunlight, or a patch of action anywhere in an otherwise calm sea, don't go in the water. Nature's food chain is in process, and there's a chance that the apex predator that inhabits the very top of that chain is out hunting, too.

Don't go in the water if you're bleeding—at all, from anything, anywhere on your body. The same salt water that may heal your cut or wound will carry away the scent of your blood. The sensory apparati of sharks are so finely tuned that they can receive and analyze the tiniest bits of blood imaginable and can direct the shark to home in on the source of the blood from far, far away.

Blood is not the only attractant that emanates from us humans; we emit sounds, smells, pressure waves, and electromagnetic fields—all of which a shark can detect. That shouldn't surprise you: you know that your dog or cat hears and sees in spectral ranges far beyond ours, so why shouldn't a shark? After all, sharks have been around, and very successful, for scores of millions of years longer than cats, dogs, and people.

Don't swim or surf in water near seal or sea lion colonies. The playful and alluring pinnipeds are the prime (and favorite) food source for, among others, great white sharks. A surfer on a board appears, when seen from below, indistinguishable from a sea lion that has come up for a breath of air. Great whites are, by nature, ambushers; they prefer to blindside their prey, attacking from below and behind, and with such speed and force that they sometimes bite through surfer *and* surfboard before they realize they've made a mistake.

Don't go swimming at dawn, dusk, or night. Many sharks—tigers, for example—come into the shallows at night to feed. On some islands, locals swear that sharks can tell when six o'clock in the evening comes along, for that's when fins can be seen crisscrossing the bay or cruising along the beach. Dim light, furthermore, decreases a shark's vision, forcing it to rely on its other senses and thus increasing the chances of a random bite.

The same holds true for swimming in turbid or murky water. A shark may sense nearby movement of a warm-blooded animal that it can't see and may decide to bite as a test of edibility.

Don't swim alone, and don't swim far from shore or other

people. As a lone swimmer you are vulnerable prey—and the farther you are from rescue if something untoward does happen, the lower your chances of survival.

Don't go swimming where people are fishing from boats. They've probably put bait in the water, or even chum, which is a mixture of blood, oil, guts, and fish bits. (Even if you're not set upon by a shark, you'll stink for days, especially your hair.)

Finally, and most obvious, don't go swimming in areas where sharks are known to congregate or feed: steep drop-offs, where tide and current sweep prey to waiting sharks; the passes in tropical lagoons where, every six hours, the change of tide brings new feeding patterns to the entire chain of wildlife in the water; channels into harbors, where fish are cleaned and remains tossed overboard by returning boats.

There are also a few don'ts for when you *do* go swimming.

Don't wear jewelry or any shiny metal in the water. It flashes and shines and can, in frothy or murky water, look to a shark like a wounded fish. A friend of mine went swimming wearing a bathing suit with a brass buckle. As he was wading out of chest-deep water, he felt something brush between his legs, and when he reached the beach he found that he'd been slashed open from thigh to knee—by something with extremely sharp teeth, either a barracuda or a small shark, for he never felt any pain. If there hadn't been a lifeguard handy to put a tourniquet around his leg, he might have bled to death.

Another friend wore a gold cross on a gold chain while he was snorkeling. A shark rushed him from below, ripped cross and chain away, and, with the same slashing bite, tore open his chin.

Don't swim in the ocean with your dog. Dogs swim with an erratic, ungainly motion that can attract curious sharks.

And don't *you* make any erratic movements, either, such as splashing, kicking, or tussling with your buddy. All of those send out signals that say, *wounded prey . . . worth investigating.*

Despite all these cautions, it's important to remember that no matter what you do, the odds are in your favor. Whether or not a person acts with vigilance and common sense, *still* the statistical chances of being set upon by a shark remain well within the comfort zone, somewhere between slim and none.

10

What to Do When
Good Dives Go Bad

USUALLY, WHEN YOU'RE DIVING—BE IT FOR SIGHT-SEEING,
sport, or business—you don't want to see sharks, any more than
you want to meet up with a bear while you're walking in the
woods or with a pack of wolves while you're cross-country skiing.

Apex predators—the creatures at the top of the food chain
that, generally, have no natural enemies except others of their
own species (and, of course, man)—have a way of spoiling your
whole day, even if they don't chase you down and tear you to bits
in an aberrant fit of madness or hunger.

If you've had good training and/or a lot of experience as a diver,
you know how to cope with equipment failures, symptoms of the
several afflictions that can befall you under water, and other routine emergencies. ("Routine emergencies" is not an oxymoron, by
the way, not when referring to the underwater world. Running

out of air is a routine emergency: there are ways to deal with the problem, and often it is preceded by warning signs. Nonroutine emergencies strike from nowhere, are impossible to prepare for, and can cascade with unbelievable speed into disaster.)

No matter how experienced or well trained you are, however, you can never be completely prepared for the sudden appearance of one or more aggressive sharks. The reason? Here it comes again: *no matter how much we think we know, the truth is, none of us knows for certain what any shark will or won't do in a given situation.*

Always remember that the shark is on its home range, and you are the intruder. Think of yourself as a trespasser in a yard posted with signs warning BEWARE OF SHARKS.

And if you see a shark, or sharks, try to keep it in view while you decide what to do next.

There are some cardinal rules for divers, but none of them is a guarantee. Here are some that, to me, make the most practical sense:

Rule #1: If you're diving on a reef and you see a shark, any shark, and it begins to behave erratically—shaking its head, hunching its back, lowering its pectoral fins—you're probably being shown a territorial threat display, a warning to *scram*. Take it seriously. Slowly and calmly retreat. Get out of the water if possible, but at least get away from the area and to a part of the reef where you can find shelter on one or two sides. In my experience, all but the largest sharks will avoid a direct, head-on, frontal assault on a scuba diver.

Rule #2: If you're diving with a group, stay together and tighten up your formation. As a group you demonstrate size, strength, and confidence (never mind that it's a fraud; the shark doesn't know that). Don't stray alone out into open water, where you broadcast vulnerability.

Rule #3: If you're a photographer, you're carrying a camera, perhaps one housed in a hard, rugged case, which can be an effective defensive weapon. Usually, a shark that bites down on a camera housing will conclude that the entire entity associated with it—that is, you—is unpalatable.

Rule #4: If you're not a photographer, make it a habit to dive with something in your hand that can be used to fend off a nosy predator: a sawed-off ski pole, maybe, an actual shark billyclub, or something like my broomstick. Nine times out of ten, a shark that comes too close or becomes too curious for comfort can be discouraged by a tap or two on the head or body. If that doesn't do the job, a vigorous jab often will.

Rule #5: Don't dive with dolphins. They can be an irresistible temptation. Dolphins look, sound, and act friendly, and they usually are. But oftentimes they also compete with sharks for the same prey, and to an excited shark a human being can appear to be a weak or wounded dolphin.

Rule #6: Some supposed experts insist that a diver should immediately exit the water at the first sight of any large shark, particularly a tiger, hammerhead, bull, mako, or great white. To me, the generalization is too general. Every encounter between diver and shark develops a situational dynamic of its own. (I do agree, however, that a diver who can't identify the particular species of shark that has appeared—and several species closely resemble others—should err on the side of caution and head for safety.)

The tiger sharks I dove with in Australia were interested in nothing but the bait laid out for them. Luckily for me, they dismissed humans—*these* humans, at least—as of no interest.

In the Sea of Cortez I dove with vast schools of scalloped hammerheads—so many that, seen from beneath, they blocked out the sun—and not once did a single one of them express anything more than idle curiosity about us.

In deep water off Rangiroa, an atoll in the Tuamotu chain of islands in French Polynesia, photographer David Doubilet and I pursued—to dicey depths between 150 and 200 feet—five enormous great hammerheads. Great hammerheads are a species unto themselves, manifestly different from the schooling scalloped hammerheads, and these five were hefty, robust females, all fifteen feet or longer. Any one of them could have consumed either of us in two bites, but not one would pause long enough for David to take a photograph.

Rangiroa is also home to a small but healthy population of silky sharks, a particularly "sharky"-looking type of shark with a super-sleek body and a perfect shark profile. Silkies are considered dangerous to man, but I've dived with the ones around Rangiroa half a dozen times or more, and I've never had trouble with any of them. Once, through a misunderstanding of signals between David and me—I thought he was signaling me to get closer to the shark, while what he was, in fact, signaling was that he was ill and about to vomit into his regulator—I let a large silky come so close to my head that I could count the pores on its snout and see the texture of its yellowish eyeball. When at last I realized what was happening, I shrugged one of my shoulders, nudging the silky in the jaw, and it sped away.

Nor have I had trouble with any of the various kinds of bull sharks, though I know that many people—divers as well as swimmers—have. If I see a bull shark under water, I never take my eyes off it. In early September 2001, I noticed that some respected journalists and scientists were declaring that bull sharks actually *do* target human beings as food. I think the conclusion is rash and no more provable than other sweeping generalizations about any species of shark. On the other hand, I am convinced that bull sharks *are* dangerous to human beings, and they merit a greater measure of fear than most other species.

I'm just as wary of makos, though they're so fast that keeping them in sight is nearly impossible. Not only are makos the fastest sharks in the sea, and armed with a mouth full of scraggly knives, but they have a reputation for crankiness.

I've been in the water with a mako only once. It appeared as if by magic, and paused in front of cinematographer Stan Waterman, no more than two feet away. Before Stan could focus his camera, his safety diver—whose sole job is to protect the back of the cameraman—panicked and whacked the mako with his "bang stick," a steel tube fitted on one end with a twelve-gauge shotgun-shell blank and a detonating mechanism. The explosion of the gases inside the cartridge blew a hole the size of a silver dollar in the mako's head, killing it instantly, and we watched the beautiful metallic blue body swirl away into the darkness of the deep.

Stan was furious; he had discerned no danger; he had had the mako in sight at all times, and it hadn't threatened him once. The gorgeous animal had died for nothing. Stan's safety diver was abashed and apologetic.

And then, finally, there is the shark for which no amount of instruction, training, warning, or anticipation can prepare a diver:

the great white. Yes, there are a few helpful things to know, such as that you can reduce the creature's advantage by letting it know that *you* know that it sees you. Great whites are ambushers by trade, preferring to attack prey from below and behind. Theoretically, if you face down a great white, you may convince it that you're too much trouble to bother with. Theoretically.

I know an individual in South Africa who snorkels and scuba dives with great whites in the open (that is, with no cage), and he sometimes carries for protection a weighted piece of wood painted to resemble an enormous great white's head in "full gape"—mouth yawning open, upper jaw down and out in bite position. He claims that his bluff has several times deceived great whites and discouraged them from attacking him.

Still, nothing in the world can prepare the average scuba diver—or, for that matter, the average *shark* diver—for an unplanned encounter with whitey. I know it to be true, for it happened to me several years ago.

The great Bermudian polymath Teddy Tucker was asked to journey to Walker's Cay in the Bahamas, to assess a pile of ancient cannons that had been discovered on the sandy bottom. The finder of the cannons wanted Teddy's opinion as to whether the guns were signs of a shipwreck in the immediate vicinity—in which case, if the wreck appeared to be from a significant era, he might finance an archeological expedition to preserve its remains—or were merely a "dump," cannons tossed overboard centuries ago from a storm-wracked ship trying to lighten itself enough to pass over the many reefs and shoals among which it had found itself trapped. Teddy would scour the rocks and coral nearby for alluvial stones that might have been used as ballast, and he would search for bits of wood or metal and for coralline overgrowth that could signal iron, bronze, silver, or sections of a ship's skeleton concealed beneath.

I accompanied Teddy as dogsbody, bat man, porter, and companion, not because he needed me but because I knew that a trip with Teddy was an adventure guaranteed, always fascinating, often exciting, and occasionally perilous. I had already written two novels based on or inspired by escapades with Teddy, *The Deep* and *The Island,* and more were to follow.

It took him only a few dives over a couple of days to conclude that the cannons were a dump. No ship had sunk with them—no ship big enough to carry this many guns, anyway, and none right here. Perhaps the ship had lightened up enough to clear the reefs and sail on to the safety of the open sea. Perhaps it had made a few hundred yards of headway and then come to grief on another reef. Perhaps the storm had broken the ship apart, sending different sections to float away to different destinations. Perhaps the ship had made it all the way home to England or Spain or France or Holland. The cannons were of English manufacture, but in an age when everyone pillaged and used everyone else's cannons and currencies (Spanish pieces of eight were legal tender in the United States, for example, until the middle of the nineteenth century), place of origin was proof of nothing further.

Unless and until the finder decided to spend the time and lavish sums of money to search naval archives and mount a proper underwater expedition, no one would ever know for certain the fate of the hapless ship.

One day, while Teddy was examining a stretch of reef, I returned to the cannons, intending to fan away the sand at the base of the heap of encrusted iron, in hopes of finding some small telltale sign of a wreck: an emerald ring, perhaps, or a gold chain. Something modest.

The water was clear and the visibility seemingly endless, so the cannons were in plain sight from the surface forty or fifty feet away. I remember the pile as being higher than I was tall and at least twenty-five or thirty feet long. A friend of ours was snorkeling on the surface, and he waved to me as I sank to the bottom and began to creep along the sand, fanning with my hand here and there to expose a crack or crevice that might be hiding what had, by now, become in my mind the Gem of Gems.

After a few pleasant but fruitless minutes of ambling and fanning, I heard a smacking sound from above. I looked up and saw that my snorkeling friend was slapping the surface and pointing down at me—or so it appeared. I looked at him for a moment, long enough to assure myself that he wasn't in trouble, then I waved to acknowledge him and continued on my way.

The slapping stopped, and now I heard the sound of swim fins churning through the water. I looked up and saw the snorkeler swimming—no, *racing*—toward the boat. He'd become bored, I assumed, or cold (though the water was soup warm). I kept going.

Not till much later did I learn that what he had been doing with all his noisy slapping was trying to save my life.

From his prospect high above, he had a clear and comprehensive view of the entire area: not just the cannons, but the sand plains that spread out from them on all sides. Seconds after I had begun to creep along the sand, he had seen, emerging from the gloom on the opposite side of the cannons, a great white shark. Not a big one—ten or twelve feet at most, probably a young male—but a great white shark nonetheless.

Anyone who has ever seen a great white in the water will never mistake it for any other species of shark. Seen from above, the great white has a unique profile. Its hefty, jumbo-jet fuselage is distinguished by what's called its caudal keel, a curved horizontal fin that protrudes just forward of the tail on both sides of its body. It resembles a diving plane on a submarine or a stabilizer on a ship, and it gives support to the tail, and streamlines the shark. Caudal keels exist in billfish and a few other species of sharks, but in none are they so pronounced. Seen from the side, a great white is thicker and more robust than, say, a silky; its snout is perfectly proportioned, not as sharp as a mako's, not as blunt as a tiger shark's. Seen head-on, it is broad-shouldered, neckless, its lower jaw slightly ajar and showing grabbing and tearing teeth, its upper lip looking sort of puckery, as if the upper jaw were toothless rather than home to row upon row of big, serrated triangular cutting teeth that lie relaxed, nearly horizontal, against the upper gums.

Seen from anywhere, it is a *big* shark, long and bulky—a seventeen-foot female can weigh more than two tons—and it moves with the ease and confidence of the toughest dude on the block.

My friend the snorkeler had been with us in South Australia, and he knew what he was seeing.

He told me later that from his vantage point the pile of cannons resembled an almond; he could see me swimming along the right side of the almond and the shark swimming up the left side at approximately the same speed. He calculated that the shark and I would meet at the point of the almond, as precisely as two characters in a Warner Bros. cartoon. He had slapped the water to warn me and pointed not at me but at the shark, until suddenly the thought had occurred to him that causing a ruckus on the surface might possibly attract the shark up to *him*. He figured that I, at least, had the advantage of being completely submerged and on apparently equal turf with the shark, while he, floundering on the surface, was nothing but bait. So he had departed, hastily, for the boat.

In my judgment, he did exactly the correct thing.

I, meanwhile, continued on, oblivious to everything save the phantom jewels undoubtedly nestled in the next pocket of sand between cannons, or certainly the one after that. My eyes riveted on the bottom, I had no reason to look up.

I reached the end of the pile of cannons, the point of the almond, and then I did look up, to orient myself, and at that very moment the great white reached the same spot.

We saw each other. Our eyes locked for perhaps a nanosecond, just long enough for my brain to register and recognize what my eyes were seeing and for its brain to register (I guess) shock and surprise.

I was paralyzed. The shark wasn't. It braked with its pectoral fins, like a plane with its flaps down for landing, spun completely around in its own length, and vanished in a billowy cloud of brown, which had exploded from its bowel.

I was alone, kneeling on the bottom, stunned and breathless and, within a few seconds, covered by a cloud of great-white-shark shit.

11

You Say You *Want* to Dive with Sharks?

WELL, YOU'D BETTER BE AN EXPERIENCED SCUBA DIVER.

And you'd better be guided by a veteran dive master who knows the local waters and its inhabitants very well indeed, because the sharks of one area may behave completely differently from sharks *of the same exact species* that inhabit another locale.

And you'd better be prepared to expect the unexpected and act accordingly.

And you'd better be able to suppress your habits and instincts and to react counterintuitively and instantaneously.

And you'd better be *extremely* lucky, because except in areas where feeding stations have been established and the resident sharks are accustomed to having humans in the water with them and have come to associate humans with (not *as*) food, sharks have no interest at all in hanging out with humans and, as a result, go out of their way to avoid them.

Especially scuba divers, who appear to a shark to be large, strange (they resemble no other animal it knows), alien (they emit blasts of *bubbles*), noisy (those bubbles are *loud*), possibly threatening, and definitely unappetizing.

More and more these days, at dive sites, hotels, and resorts around the world, divers want to see, be in the presence of, and photograph sharks. They're prepared to travel vast distances and pay big money to dive with sharks of all kinds, from great whites to whale sharks, blue sharks, hammerheads, duskies, and silkies.

Crusaders for the conservation of sharks, who work in opposition to international commercial interests that kill millions of sharks every year for their fins, have labored to come up with a statistic proving that a live shark is worth much more to a community, any community, than a dead one. The statistic is no more reliable than any other, but it makes the point.

Every shark killed for its fins brings a fisherman and his community somewhere between five and fifty dollars, whereas every shark that is left alive to become an attraction for diving tourists generates fifty thousand dollars a year in income for the community.

While that statistic isn't provable, there is an underlying truth to it, similar to the old adage, Give a man a fish and you feed him for a day; teach a man to fish and you feed him for a lifetime. The truth here is, tourism is the fastest-growing industry in the world; tourism can transform and save ailing, inefficient economies; diving is an important element in tourism; divers want to see sharks.

Conclusion: preserve your local sharks, and you'll attract tourist dollars, which ripple out into the rest of the island (or seaside or port or coastline) economy and support restaurants, hotels, car-rental franchises, shops, video-rental stores, and so on, ad infinitum.

For the most part, intentional diving with sharks is reasonably safe, because it is chaperoned and supervised by experts. Even the many shark-feeding enterprises that are springing up all over the world (especially in the Bahamas) are, as a rule, conducted so that the paying customers are kept out of jeopardy.

Shark feeding is, however, increasingly controversial. Scientists worry that behavioral patterns are altered in sharks that become accustomed to being fed by humans; natural behavior becomes unnatural when it is interfered with. Sharks lose part of their "sharkness." They are, in a sense, corrupted by contact with people.

Surfers, abalone divers, chambers of commerce, and seaside merchants are worried about a different, less theoretical, and more practical potential problem: the supposed danger caused by habituating sharks to being fed by humans. If certain sharks learn to associate humans with food, how will they react to the presence of humans who *don't* come bearing food? To counter that concern, operators of shark-feeding programs point out that the sharks conditioned to feeding stations tend to remain in those areas; if you make your living hunting for food and you find a place where food is given to you, why move? The sharks that occasionally maul people in the surf off bathing beaches aren't reacting to conditioning; they're chasing food.

I can't speak with authority to the first concern, though it sounds logical and serious.

With the second, however, I am intimately familiar. I was party to a pseudoscientific "experiment" long ago, and the recollection, seen with the benefit of hindsight over many years of acquired knowledge and experience, causes me some chagrin.

Shark feeding as a resort attraction was in its infancy. Scuba diving itself was still a relatively young and exotic sport. I was asked to do a TV show on Long Island in the Bahamas, where a dive master had conditioned local sharks to assemble at a certain sand hole in a reef at a certain time of day, and to expect and accept food skewered on a spear stuck in the sand and, some-times, to eat directly from his hands.

The routine called for paying customers to gather in a circle in the sand hole, surrounding the dive master, who would lure the sharks to the food. The sharks would arrive, swooping over and between the divers, and would then fight over the food. After ten or fifteen minutes, the food would be gone and the sharks would disperse, eyeballing the divers and passing near enough to give them a thrill and a chance to take a good close-up with their underwater cameras.

Not for us. Not exciting enough. We were pros. We had to go where other divers dared not. We had to test the limits. So some-body cooked up the idea of measuring the bite dynamics of the sharks, determining how many pounds of pressure per square inch a shark—in this case a variety of bull shark, as I recall—could exert with its jaws.

We built a gnathodynamometer—a seventeen-letter word for a bite meter—which was nothing more than a sandwich of two dead fish tied to a slab of pressure-sensitive plastic. The idea was that the "talent"—I and a photogenic young Ph.D. candidate named Clarisse—would hand-feed the sandwich to as many sharks as possible, after which we'd determine from the depth of the tooth marks the pressure the sharks' jaws had exerted.

The first gnathodynamometer was an instant casualty. No one had paused to consider what would happen if two, three, or more sharks went for it at once. Clarisse and I held it out to a single shark, which swam between us, opened its mouth, seized the sandwich, and was instantly dive-bombed by three other sharks. Knocked aside, we watched helplessly as the sharks swarmed in a ball of fury, tore the fish to shreds, and swam away with the plastic.

We tried again, this time while a dive master distracted most of the sharks with their usual food. One shark detached from the group, cruised over the bottom toward us, and lunged upward for the gnathodynamometer. But its tail disturbed so much sand, which billowed in a cloud around us, that it couldn't see where it was going, and instead of biting the sandwich it grabbed a yellow steel-cased strobe light, which it gnawed and worried until, convinced that the light wasn't appetizing, it gave up and swam away.

It took several days of trial and error for us to get the shots we sought, but succeed at last we did, and without loss of digit or limb. When the shooting was over, our eleven-year-old son, Clayton, who had watched the action through a face mask at the surface, asked us to take him down to see a shark—if any were still around.

Without thinking, Wendy and I said, "Sure." Clayton had been diving for three years; he was careful and knowledgeable, and he obeyed instructions. We knew that most of the sharks had gone, and we were confident that, between us, we could shepherd him safely to and from the bottom.

We checked all his gear, refreshed him on all the precautions, and went overboard off the stern. I went first and sank straight to the bottom; Clayton came next; Wendy followed.

We three knelt on the sand and looked around at the empty blue, hoping to see a single shark swimming placidly in the distance.

We never saw the first shark arrive. It bore down upon us from above, passed quickly before us, and began to circle ten, perhaps fifteen, feet away.

Two more sharks arrived and joined the circle. Wendy and I closed in on Clayton and looked into each other's eyes. Simultaneously, we recognized the gross error we had just committed: by jumping into the water and descending into the same sand hole where the feeding ritual took place every day, we had, essentially, given cues to trained animals. And they had responded.

Three more sharks swam in from the gloom; other gray shadows began to appear in the distance.

Soon there were thirteen sharks circling us, expectant but calm . . . at least for the time being.

We had no food to give them. We couldn't hold up our end of the implicit bargain.

How long would it take the first shark to understand that it had been betrayed, that the rules had been broken? How would it react?

Were they all well fed? Had one or two perhaps not gotten their share during the feeding?

Were all of these thoughts—tripping over one another to crowd into the chaos of my head—nothing more than ludicrous anthropomorphizing?

All I knew for certain was that we had no time to wait for answers. Already a couple of the sharks were exhibiting signs of . . . not agitation, not excitement . . . the only word that came to me was *impatience*.

One shark shivered visibly; a ripple traveled the length of its hard, sleek, steel gray body. Another began to swim in spurts, speeding up and slowing down.

I couldn't tell what Clayton was feeling. He knelt motionless, now and then turning his head to watch a particular shark but mostly letting the parade pass before his eyes. Wendy and I had a hand on each of his arms, as one of us always did in any remotely scary circumstance, to ensure that he wouldn't, in panic, suddenly rush for the surface, forgetting his training, and risk becoming a victim of any one of several unhappy accidents.

I looked up at the boat, which was clearly visible directly overhead some thirty feet above us. Then I made contact with Wendy's eyes and told her (as best I could) that I had come to a decision and that she should do exactly as I did. She seemed to— and indeed, she did—understand.

I tapped Clayton to get his attention. He looked up at me, obviously excited, obviously afraid. His eyes, seen through the distortion of mask and water, were the size of extra-large eggs. I made the "okay" sign to him—a circle formed by thumb and forefinger—then touched his mask and mine, saying, *Watch me, do as I do.* He shot me the "okay" sign.

Together, we three rose off our knees and stood on the sand.

The sharks took notice of our movement. Though they didn't change their pace, they closed ranks just a bit, shrinking the diameter of the circle.

Wendy and I faced each other and surrounded Clayton. My right hand held her left. With my left hand, I mimed counting down from three to zero. She closed her eyes for a second, then nodded.

I counted down, and at zero we filled our lungs with compressed air, pressed the purge valves on our regulator mouthpieces, and kicked off the bottom.

A thick, noisy column of bubbles filled the space between us as, shielding Clayton with our bodies, we rose toward the boat, exhaling slowly, fighting the urge to hurry, staying always beneath the last of our bubbles, to prevent any rogue air bubble from being trapped in some tiny space in our lungs, whence it might burst free and become an embolus.

The ploy was elementary and by no means guaranteed to succeed. In general, sharks dislike bubbles. In general, they stay away from loud, erratic bursts of bubbles. Engineers have built bubble "curtains" in attempts to protect beaches, but they've proven to be unreliable.

My hope was that by huddling together and blasting bubbles from our regulators, we would appear to the sharks as an infernal machine worthy of not even a close inspection, let alone an exploratory bite.

Not once did I look down, but Clayton did, and later he told me that the circle of sharks had broken apart as soon as we left and that individual sharks had begun to follow us upward.

We broke through the surface, and in a single motion Wendy and I propelled Clayton up onto the swim step. Next Wendy hauled herself onto the little platform, while I hung off, prepared to kick at any shark that made a run at her legs.

One shark had followed us nearly to the surface. Now it circled tightly just below my feet. I couldn't turn away to climb aboard the boat; I had to keep watching it, in case it should lunge for me.

I hoped that hands would reach down from above and haul me aboard, and Wendy did, in fact, grab the neck of my tank to keep me from drifting away. But she didn't have the strength to lift me and tank and weights and wetsuit clear of the water.

After perhaps a minute, the shark turned away and swam off, and I shucked my tank and pulled myself into the boat.

Wendy and I looked at our son. He had taken off his tank and was shedding his wetsuit. He was trembling, and his lips were blue, from cold or fear or . . .

We had no words for each other. We had almost lost . . . we *could* have lost . . . we were both guilty of . . . how could we have . . . ?

"Wow!" Clayton shouted. "I've never been so scared in my life."

"I know," I began. "I—"

"Can I go again? Can I? Please?"

At eleven years old, he was immortal.

We said no.

12

Teach Your Children Well
Some Shark Facts and a Story

YOU MAY ALREADY HAVE DISCOVERED THAT YOUR CHILDREN, especially your male children, know more about sharks than you do.

As a corollary to my conviction that all kids are fascinated by sharks or dinosaurs, I believe that sharks have one particular advantage over dinosaurs: they still exist; they're still visible in the wild, still photographable, filmable, and videotapeable. The Discovery Channel's "Shark Week" has become a popular and successful institution. Most broadcast and cable-TV channels have access to a huge archive of shark footage, and digital technology has so quickly become so good and so inexpensive that nowadays, as soon as discoveries of any kind are made—whether of new species or new behaviors—they're recorded and broadcast, with ratings success all but guaranteed.

The movie *Jaws* appears on television somewhere in the world nearly every day of the year, and it continues to draw audiences.

The eternal verity endures: kids love sharks.

Still, it's possible that there are children who don't know much about sharks. So for them, and for their parents, here is a brief primer on sharks, "true facts," if you will, absent hype, gore, and sensation:

- Sharks are fish, but they're not like other fish, because they have no real bones. Sharks and the other members of the elasmobranch family of sea creatures, including skates and rays, have skeletons made of cartilage, the same stuff we have in our knees and other joints and in our noses and ears.

- Sharks are some of the oldest animals on earth. They've been around much longer than man or any other mammals—probably as much as four hundred million years—and they haven't changed very much in at least the last thirty million.

- Sharks have always been among nature's most perfect creations, efficiently performing the functions nature programmed them to do: eat, swim, and reproduce.

- There are hundreds of different kinds of sharks. Nobody knows exactly how many because (1) new species are being discovered all the time, and (2) we have explored so very little of the oceans that cover 70 percent of our planet's surface that we really have no notion of the true nature and variety of all that lives down there.

- Sharks range over all extremes of size, looks, and appetites. They include the whale shark—the biggest fish in the sea, which can grow to fifty feet long and weigh many tons but is completely harmless to people and eats only the tiniest of sea creatures—and the cookie-cutter shark, which grows to only about a foot and a half but inflicts terrible wounds on much bigger animals, like other sharks and dolphins, by using its razor-sharp teeth to remove large chunks of flesh.

- Sharks include the largest meat-eating fish in the sea— the great white, which has attacked and eaten human beings—and some of the smallest meat eaters, too, like the so-called cigar shark, which fits in the palm of your hand, and the dwarf shark, which only grows to ten inches long.

- Sharks also include some of the weirdest-looking fish in the sea. The horn shark, which grows to roughly three feet long, has a face that resembles a pig's and teeth that are flat, not pointed, that it uses to crush the animals it eats. The wobbegong shark is camouflaged to be invisible against a coral reef. It never bothers people ... unless people bother it. A friend of mine was bitten by a wobbegong when she put her finger on it to show me how well it was hidden.

- Sharks are very important to maintaining the balance of nature in the sea. As apex predators, those at the very top of the food chain, they keep the numbers of other animals in check and healthy, culling populations of the old, the weak, and the sick.

- Scientists suspect that sharks perform several other important functions in the sea, but they don't know exactly what those functions are because they've had so little time and money with which to study sharks. Unlike whales, with which people can identify because they do a lot of humanlike things, sharks do not breathe air, do not nurse their young, do not communicate with one another in an audible "language," and do not interrelate with humans at all. Consequently, there has not been much popular effort to get to know them.

- Since the first human ventured onto the sea thousands of years ago, sharks have always been perceived as dangerous, sometimes even evil, and so there hasn't been much pressure on governments to spend money to study them. Most people believe that the best way to deal with sharks is to stay away from them. Some even believe that "the only good shark is a dead shark," a belief that springs from a combination of fear and ignorance.

- Unfortunately, sharks have turned out to be *very* vulnerable to destruction, and possibly even extinction, by man. Prized for their fins (for soup), their meat (especially makos), their skins (for leather), their teeth (for jewelry), and their organs and cartilage (for medicines), sharks have in recent years been so heavily overfished that some species may never recover.

- The downfall of sharks may, ironically, be hastened by the same qualities for which nature created them. Because apex predators are, by definition, at the top of the food chain, nothing preys on them except larger versions of themselves and, sometimes, killer whales. To maintain ecological balance, the numbers of each species of apex predator—be it grizzly bear, lion, tiger, or shark—must remain low; nature assured this by designing these animals to breed relatively late in life and relatively seldom and to produce relatively few young that will survive to adulthood. Great white sharks, for example, have small litters (often only one or two), but each pup is born large (four or five feet long), fully formed, fully armed, and ready to rumble. In other species there is cannibalism in utero, so few young are born alive; still others pup many live young, but they're so small and vulnerable to being eaten by other creatures that only the fittest (and the luckiest) survive.

- Finally, in their appearance, their efficiency, and the striking evidence that they're living examples of Charles Darwin's concept of adaptive radiation, sharks are—to me, anyway—among the most beautiful of all the creatures on earth.

Here is a story I wrote about sharks, to explain how they function in the complex chain of life by which we are all—each and every living thing on planet Earth—inextricably linked together.

The Day All the Sharks Died

Once upon a time, there was a seaside village whose people lived in harmony with nature.

They made their living from the sea. They caught fish on the reef that protected the village from the full fury of ocean storms.

They gathered clams and oysters, mussels and scallops from the bays and coves and inlets. Some they ate themselves; some they sold to people in other towns and villages, from whom they bought necessities like lightbulbs and clothing and radios and refrigerators and fuel for their boats and cars.

Their biggest business, which employed the most people and brought in the most money, was lobster fishing. Professional lobstermen owned special boats and had special licenses that permitted them to set a certain number of pots or traps to catch lobsters. The law permitted the fishermen to catch only lobsters that were too big to pass through a special ring, which meant that they were old enough to have bred and had young of their own. Smaller lobsters were put back in the sea to live and grow, as were female lobsters carrying eggs.

Everyone worked together to maintain a healthy, stable population of lobsters, for many people's livelihoods depended on them: not only the fishermen who caught them and the mates who worked on the boats but the wholesalers on the docks who bought the lobsters, processed them, and packed them up for shipping; the truckers who took the lobsters to stores and restaurants up and down the coast; the men and women who worked at the restaurants where lobsters were served; the businesses that cleaned the linen used in the restaurants; the bankers who financed the businesses; and so on, like ripples spreading from the splash of a stone dropped in a pond.

So valuable were the lobsters to the people of the village that very few of the villagers ate lobster themselves. Eating lobster, they said, made them feel as if they were eating the money in their pockets. That may not make sense to you or me, but it was the way the people felt. They'd eat clams they caught themselves, or fish they caught themselves, but not lobsters.

The villagers grew vegetables in their gardens and fruit on the trees planted many years ago on the hillsides behind the village.

A small colony of sea lions lived on a rocky point of land that joined the breakwater at the mouth of the harbor, and in the springtime tourists from other towns would come to the village and have lunch at one of the restaurants on the harbor, just for the fun of watching the newborn sea lion pups playing with one another, or learning how to swim and hunt for food, or sunning themselves on the warm rocks.

There always seemed to be exactly enough sea lions to keep the colony healthy, never so many that they had to fight for food with one another or with the village fishermen, never so few that inbreeding became a problem and pups were born dead or deformed.

The villagers' garbage was collected by big trucks that took it away to dumps somewhere far inland. The sewage from their showers, toilets, and washing machines ran into pipes buried

along the road in front of the village and was carried to treat-
ment plants that removed the sludge and cleansed the water.

They did not think much, or worry at all, about the great
numbers and variety of creatures that lived in the sea. The sea
and all its living things seemed infinite, indestructible, eternal.

Nor did they worry about the predators that lived in the sea.
They knew that sharks patrolled the reef and the deep water
beyond, but never—not in living memory or in village lore—
had anyone ever been bitten, let alone killed, by a shark.

The villagers had, of course, been taught from birth to
respect the sea and the animals in it, so they took sensible precautions. Even on the scorching-hot days of summer no one
swam at dawn or at dusk, when sharks were known to feed on
the reef and when, once in a great while, a dorsal fin could be
spotted slicing the flat-calm surface of the water in the harbor.

They never swam near fishermen, or wherever bait was in
the water. They never swam if they saw fish feeding or birds
feeding on fish. No one swam or snorkeled or dove or scalloped
with a fresh cut or an open sore.

Nobody fished for sharks because none of the locals liked
shark meat and there wasn't a market for it anywhere nearby,
and if a fisherman caught a shark by accident, on a line or in a
net, he'd let it go. Nobody in the village ever killed anything
just for the sake of killing. Except bugs. And spiders, now and
then, although the elementary-school teacher had made it a
personal crusade to teach every child in her care how important spiders were in keeping down the numbers of, among
other things, bugs.

One day people noticed a big boat—big enough, in fact, to

be considered a ship—lingering not far offshore. Smaller boats were put overboard from the ship, and they cruised up and down the reef, doing something or other.

Village fishermen who had gotten close enough to the ship to read its name couldn't remember it or pronounce it, because it was stenciled on the ship's bow and fantail not only in a foreign language but in an alphabet nobody could decipher.

The one peculiar thing about the ship that fishermen could describe was that on her stern were two very, very big—gigantic, even—spools, each of which looked like it could hold at least a mile's worth of thick, strong fishing line. And visible in the coils of line were baited hooks, too many to count.

When the people in the village awoke on the morning of the third day, the ship was gone. Everything seemed to be okay; nothing looked different.

There was no way anyone could know that, over the past two days, their village had been murdered.

The first sign that something was wrong was discovered by fishermen who went out to the reef. Scattered over the bottom, in the reef and on the sand, they saw the dead bodies of sharks. (Because sharks do not have swim bladders like other fish, when they die they do not float. They sink to the bottom.) They saw that the sharks had not only been killed, they had been mutilated: their fins had been slashed off—dorsal fins from their backs, caudal fins from their tails, pectoral fins from their sides—and the sharks had been thrown back into the sea to bleed to death or drown.

The fishermen's first reaction was anger: so *this* was what the foreign ship had been doing offshore, killing our sharks and taking their fins to sell to the people who make shark-fin soup, an expensive delicacy.

Their second reaction was frustration: what could they do about this thievery? They knew the answer: nothing. The ship had come from a foreign land, and from experience the villagers knew that their local police and wardens and marshals had no power over foreign vessels.

Their third reaction was resignation: well, the shark populations will rebound. Sharks from other regions up and down the coast will come here. Nature will stay in balance.

What they didn't know was that there *were* no sharks in other regions up and down the coast. The big ship and the boats it carried had worked the entire coastline, taking all the sharks from all the reefs and using the long lines on the huge spools that sat on the stern of the big boat to catch the open-water sharks, the big ones that fed on sea lions.

For the first few weeks, nothing seemed much different. Fish and lobsters were caught and sold, money was earned and money was spent, and life continued as before.

Then fishermen began to notice that they were catching fewer lobsters in the pots. Slowly at first, then more rapidly, the number of lobsters was declining. Often lobster fishermen found in their pots not lobsters but octopuses. They had never paid attention to octopuses before. Now the octopuses seemed to be everywhere.

Within a month or two, the villagers realized that the number of sea lions had increased, too, especially young ones. As the sea lion population grew, the number of fish caught by the village's fishermen declined. In itself, this was no mystery: sea lions subsist on fish, so as their numbers increased, they took more and more fish from the sea.

The mystery was, why had the sea lion population exploded?

Soon there were so many sea lions that they outgrew their rocky point and spread back toward the village. Some took up residence on docks, some on boats moored in the harbor. Normally friendly and playful, the sea lions were not accustomed to being forced to move from their perches, and some showed irritation—even aggression—toward the people who approached them.

Since sea lions poop wherever they please, boat owners found the decks and cockpits of their boats soiled and stinking.

When the wind blew toward shore, the stink wafted into the village and made dining an unpleasant experience. Restaurants lost customers; waiters and waitresses were laid off, and some had to move away to find new jobs, leaving houses and apartments vacant.

Lobster catches continued to drop. To make up for lost income, lobstermen wanted to raise the price-per-pound they were paid for the lobsters they did catch, but the wholesalers refused: catches elsewhere in the country had not declined, so the overall number of lobsters available was, more or less, the same as usual. If the price of local lobsters rose, markets and restaurants would simply import their lobsters from elsewhere.

Most lobster fishermen had borrowed money from banks to pay for their boats. Some had borrowed to pay for their homes as well. The loans were to be paid back over many years, but payments were due every month. Now, with their income so low, they couldn't make the monthly payments.

The banks were as fair and generous as they could be, but their revenues were down, too, and so eventually they had no choice but to take the lobster boats from the fishermen and try to sell them to someone somewhere else.

Every one of these decisions and actions became a new stone dropped into the pond: ripples spread, affecting businesses and men and women and their families for miles and miles around.

And always the question lingered: *why?* What had gone so terribly wrong so terribly fast?

By the time the answer came the following summer, the village was, by almost every measure, dying. The signs of its demise were visible to anyone: the words FOR SALE printed, stenciled, painted, scribbled, and hung on houses, boats, shops, restaurants, cars in driveways, and lawn mowers on lawns; the silent streets; the nearly empty harbor; and the vast, uncountable population of sea lions that, by now, inhabited every square inch of waterfront property in the village.

All the sea lions were unnaturally lean. Many were scrawny to the point of starvation. There were not enough fish in the harbor and on the reef to feed them all. Only those strong enough to swim far out to sea and dive very deep were able to feed themselves, and even they expended so much energy catching food that they could barely keep themselves nourished; they had no extra to feed to their young. And so, as nature had programmed them to do, mother sea lions let their pups starve to death; their natural duty was to keep themselves alive so they could breed new litters of pups every year; instinct told them that the cycle of life would eventually turn from scarcity to plenty, and soon there would be enough food for themselves *and* their pups.

For now, though, they had to let their pups die, and the bodies of the dead young sea lions rotted on the rocks and washed around in the shallows, not even fulfilling their own natural function of providing nourishment for the larger predators because, you see, there *were* no predators left alive.

It was a high school student working on a paper who discovered what had killed the village, and her discovery wasn't even very complicated. Anyone could have made it; the reason no one had was that no one had known how and where to look. Once the student began to look, answers came quickly.

She examined the food chain in the sea when the village had been thriving. At the top were the sharks. Some sharks preyed on the fish on the reef; all sharks preyed on octopuses. Octopuses, in fact, were one of the sharks' favorite foods, which was one of the things that kept octopuses from overrunning the reef. Octopuses lay thousand and thousands of eggs at one time, but nature does not intend that all of them will survive. Many are destined to become food for small fish, many for larger fish, many for sharks. When the sharks had disappeared, the student discovered, the octopus population had boomed out of natural proportion, and many more octopuses than normal were growing to adulthood.

Now, one of an octopus's favorite foods is lobster. An octopus will trap a lobster with one or more of its eight powerful arms, squeeze it to death and crack it apart with its arms, and then eat it with its powerful beak. Even small octopuses can catch and eat small lobsters—lobsters too small and young to have had a chance to reproduce—so when the sea around the village became overpopulated with octopuses, the lobster population suddenly crashed.

Very soon there were no more lobsters for the fishermen to catch.

Normally, other sharks—larger ones, including great whites—preyed upon the sea lion colony, taking the weak, the sick, the malformed, and the vulnerable, leaving only the strong and healthy sea lions to maintain the colony.

When those sharks were killed by the big fishing ship, there were no predators left to control the growth of the sea lion colony. And since sharks are not only predators but scavengers as well, even the dead sea lions were not recycled into the food chain but left to rot and become host to flies and other carriers of disease.

The most discouraging discovery the student made was that, in all likelihood, the village would never recover. The damage done was irreversible and permanent. Although no entire *species* of sharks had yet been fished to extinction, what had been done to the village was being done to thousands upon thousands of towns and villages all over the world, so shark populations were being devastated worldwide. Because sharks breed late in life (some species not until they are twenty-five or thirty years old) and produce so few young, of which even fewer survive to maturity, their former numbers would never return.

The marine food chain had been altered forever.

The student turned in her paper, and she received a good grade. She would have received the highest grade, but her teacher said the report lacked solutions for the problems the student had discovered.

But there *are* no solutions, replied the student.

Nonsense, said the teacher. There are always solutions, for everything.

In this case, however, the teacher was wrong. He did not recognize the truly significant discovery the student had made: that nature is not invulnerable, the ocean is not infinite and eternal, and that now, for the first time in history, mankind has the power to destroy the ocean that gives life to the planet that gives life to us. We can actually affect the fundamental functioning of the earth, altering the mechanisms that give us the air we breathe, the water we drink, and the food we eat.

What the student knew in her heart but was loath to believe and afraid to articulate was that unless mankind changes its ways—and soon—we have all begun a leisurely stroll down a seductively gentle slope to eventual self-destruction.

All this she had learned by studying the events that followed the day when the sharks died in the waters off the seaside village that used to live in harmony with nature.

PART III

13

Dangerous to Man?
Moray Eels, Killer Whales, Barracudas, and Other Creatures We Fear

WE HUMANS LIVE ON THE EDGE OF THE WORLD'S LARGEST primal wilderness, the ocean. We venture onto and into it for recreation, relaxation, and exercise, without appreciating the fact that the ocean is the hunting ground for most of the living things on planet Earth.

No matter how peaceful the sea may seem on a warm and sunny day, it is in fact always—*always!*—a brutal world governed by two basic rules: kill or be killed, and eat or be eaten.

Sharks are by no means the only predators that haunt the wilds outside our back door; they're just the biggest and most spectacular. Every living thing, of every size and shape conceivable, possesses weapons with which to defend itself and tools with which to feed itself, and when we enter into alien territory—startling, frightening, or, occasionally, tempting creatures that are minding their own business and behaving as nature has programmed them to behave—we shouldn't be surprised if we get into trouble.

Many years ago, the late Roger Caras wrote a book I liked titled *Dangerous to Man,* in which he examined many of the animals perceived as threatening to humans and explained why, and in what circumstances, each one should or shouldn't be feared. His underlying premise, of course, was that *no* animal is dangerous to man if man will leave it alone. Believing that Caras's book could be translated into an excellent series of informative half hours for television, some friends and I almost succeeded in getting the project made. It was not to be, but the premise of the book is still valid. In the next pages I'll describe the marine animals most commonly thought of as being dangerous to man. I hope you'll conclude, as I have, that the animal *truly* most dangerous to man is man.

The list that follows is incomplete, for it includes only the animals of which I or friends of mine have personal knowledge, or which I've studied so much for so long that I think I know them pretty well. (For technical details about some of the creatures, I have drawn liberally from Richard Ellis's superb *Encyclopedia of the Sea.*)

Moray Eels

There are a great many kinds, colors, and sizes of moray eels, most of which live in tropical and subtropical waters. Morays range in size from under a foot to nearly ten feet long, and I know from experience that a seven-footer—as big around as a football and displaying its long, white, needlelike fangs—is as scary-looking a monster as there is under water.

A significant contributor to its frightening appearance is its manner of respiring. Its mouth opens and closes constantly, which forces oxygen-rich water over its gills but which also, when accentuated by its wide, blank, maniacally staring eyes, makes the eel look as if it can't wait to rip your head off.

Morays aren't poisonous, but their bites can carry so much toxic bacteria that they might as well be. They're scavengers as well as predators, and they have no aversion to rotten flesh. A moray bite is usually ragged (thus difficult to suture), exceedingly painful, and quick to become infected. It is also usually a mistake: the eel confuses a human digit for a piece of food. Usually, that is. But not always.

David Doubilet, the incomparable underwater photographer with whom I've worked for more than twenty years, was once severely bitten on the hand by a yellowish-colored moray off Hawaii. The eel, he says, literally charged him—zoomed out of its hole, bit him, and went home. The wound not only took forever to heal but left considerable residual damage to David's hand.

Al Giddings, the underwater cinematographer who worked on *Titanic* and *The Abyss*, was bitten by a moray in 1976 during the filming of the movie based on my novel *The Deep*, of which he was codirector of underwater photography. Columbia Pictures had built a two-million-gallon tank to contain its underwater sets in Bermuda and stocked it with live animals, including a shark and some eels, one of which took a liking to one of Al's toes. Al kept his toe, but the wound became infected immediately, and he lost some diving time.

There's no reason for swimmers, snorkelers, or scuba divers to get into trouble with morays, and there are only a couple of circumstances in which people do get bitten.

The eels live in cavelets, crannies, and holes in reefs, and an incautious diver who goes poking around—searching for lobsters, perhaps—risks having a probing hand mistaken for a fish, seized, gnawed on, and shredded.

Another risky business involves morays that have been conditioned to accept and be fed by humans. As dive masters and other sea-savvy folks know, conditioning is not the same as taming, and eels, fish, sharks, and other marine creatures (except for some of the mammals) *cannot be tamed*. No one should ever try to treat a moray eel like a pet.

The danger in conditioning morays is rarely to the conditioner or the conditioner's customers. They, after all, play by established rules: they arrive at the dive site, bringing fish scraps or other savory dead things for the eel (or eels, though to deal with more than two at once is to court serious danger); the eel emerges from its hole, expecting to be fed; it is fed; it permits itself to be touched and handled; sometimes, if the ritual has been repeated enough times that it has become imprinted as part of the eel's repertoire, it will hunt for morsels concealed on the diver's person, slithering in and out of his buoyancy-compensator vest, between his legs, around his neck.

For the paying customer, the performance looks truly impressive, and, in fact, it *is*.

The most remarkable morays I've ever seen lived on a reef off Grand Cayman. They had been conditioned by Wayne and Ann Hasson, who at the time ran a successful diving operation in the Cayman Islands. (You'll have noticed by now that I persist in using the word *conditioned* instead of *trained*. It's because I'm not certain that what the eels are taught to do constitutes training:

they don't jump through hoops or play volleyball or do anything else they're not accustomed to doing. They eat—though, granted, in an unnatural way, that is, from the hands of humans, whom they have been taught to tolerate and, to an extent, trust. Is that training? I don't think so; I think it's conditioning.)

Wayne and Ann had arbitrarily anthropomorphized the two green morays into a heterosexual couple named Waldo and Waldeen. Both were enormous: six and a half or seven feet long (longer than I am tall, that much I know for sure), at least a foot high, and as thick as a large honeydew or a small watermelon.

David Doubilet and I were doing a story on the Caymans for *National Geographic,* and Wendy and our daughter, Tracy—both certified divers—had come along to enjoy a couple of weeks of the best diving in the Caribbean.

Tracy has always had a mystical, almost spooky, ability to communicate with animals both terrestrial and marine. I don't mean "communicate" in the Dr. Dolittle sense; she doesn't talk to animals. Nor do I mean it in the Shirley MacLaine sense; she doesn't channel Amenhotep through turtles. She and animals merely appear to trust each other.

That kind of trust isn't uncommon for humans to have with dogs, cats, horses, and other mammals. But with *fish*? I have seen big groupers come to Tracy—while avoiding every other human in the area—and almost snuggle up to her. I'll forever retain a vision of her in the Caymans, walking slowly along the bottom, with two groupers swimming beside her, one under each arm.

The only person I know with a greater affinity than Tracy for marine creatures is Valerie Taylor, the legendary Australian photographer, diver, and marine conservationist, who truly *is* spooky—off the scale. I believe that Valerie could wordlessly convince any fish, eel, or dolphin to fetch her newspaper, pick up her laundry, and wash the car.

One day, Ann Hasson introduced Tracy to one of the giant green morays—Waldeen, I think—and when the eel had been fed and stroked by Ann, it took immediately to Tracy, snaking all around her, in and out of her buoyancy-compensator vest, seeming not to be seeking food so much as getting acquainted. Tracy never moved, except to raise her arms slowly to give Waldeen another platform around which to slither.

After a few moments, the eel calmly slid away from Tracy and returned to its home in the reef. We all puttered around for another minute or two, then prepared to move on. When I signaled to Tracy to follow us, however, she shook her head, calmly but definitely saying no.

I was bewildered: what did she mean, *no*? What did she plan to do, stand there all day? Then I saw her point downward with one index finger, and I looked at her feet, and there was Waldeen, halfway out of the reef, with its huge, gaping jaws around Tracy's ankle. The eel's head was moving gently back and forth, its jaws throbbing open and closed on my daughter's bare flesh.

Waldeen was mouthing Tracy, the way a Labrador retriever will mouth your hand to get you to play with it. Labradors, though, are known for having a "soft mouth"; moray eels aren't.

Tracy's expression was serene. Clearly, she was neither hurt nor afraid. She stayed still. I stayed still, too, paralyzed with fear and wondering what I'd do if I suddenly vomited into my mask.

The eel played with Tracy's ankle for perhaps another thirty seconds, then withdrew into the reef.

We moved on.

When we returned to the Cayman Islands a couple of years later, I learned that both Waldo and Waldeen were gone. One had been caught and killed by local fishermen—illegally, of course—and the other was said to have vanished. I'd bet that he or she, whichever it was, had been killed, too, for the most prominent danger attendant on conditioning eels to trust humans is not to the humans but to the eels. Their fate is familiar and almost inevitable; I've seen it happen all over the world, from the Cayman Islands in the Caribbean to the Tuamotu Islands in French Polynesia.

An eel is conditioned to associate humans with food. Sometimes the betrayal is simple. A spearfisher will descend to the reef, maybe carrying food, maybe not. The eel will emerge from its den. The fisher kills it. More often, though, the eel's demise is more complex.

Once there lived a big moray eel in a large coral head inside the lagoon of the Rangiroa Atoll in the Tuamotus. Our son Christopher used to like to visit the eel, to watch it as it waited in ambush in the shelter of the coral. Now and then he'd see the eel dart out of its hole and, with blurring speed, snatch and kill a passing fish. Christopher kept his distance from the eel, for though local laws forbade the feeding of morays, it was common knowledge that glass-bottom-boat operators from cruise ships would send snorkelers down with food, to draw eels out of their holes for the entertainment of their passengers. Christopher didn't carry food with him, and he didn't want the eel to make any false assumptions about him.

News came one afternoon that a swimmer had been badly bitten by a moray eel and had had to be evacuated by air to a hospital in Tahiti. By coincidence, we were scheduled to go out into the lagoon that day. When we reached the coral head, Christopher put on mask, fins, and snorkel and dove down to see his friend, the eel.

The eel had been speared, just behind the head. It was still alive, struggling to retreat into its hole, but the steel shaft that had gone clean through its body now protruded a foot or more from either side, stopping the eel from retreating.

Christopher hung in the water, helpless, and watched the eel die.

We heard later what had happened. A snorkeler had happened by and seen the eel waiting in the opening of its hole. She had approached very close to the eel, which—thinking she was bearing food, like other humans who came so near—came out of its hole prepared to feed.

When the woman gave it nothing, the eel pursued her, conditioned to associate humans with food. The flesh the eel saw looked like food but was, in fact, the woman's hand.

I'm sure you can finish the story yourself. The eel was deemed too dangerous to live, and a diver was dispatched to dispatch it. In truth, of course, the eel had only been obeying the conditioning imprinted upon it by humans.

The single strangest experience I've ever had with moray eels occurred in the Galápagos Islands, where I first went in 1987 to appear in a television show for John Wilcox. Stan Waterman was one of two underwater cameramen. The other was Howard Hall, one of the finest wildlife filmmakers working anywhere in the world today. Paul Humann, author of many fish-identification books and an expert still photographer who had spent hundreds, if not thousands, of hours under water in the Galápagos, was "co-talent" with me; he would act as my guide and docent for the cameras.

Before the simple two-week shoot was over, all three of them were to escape death and serious injury by the narrowest of margins: Stan and Paul by being lost in the open ocean at twilight and, another day, by being set upon suddenly by a large school of very aggressive small sharks; Howard and Paul, after Stan and I had departed, when the boat we had chartered crashed into an island and sank in the middle of the night. (The boat had been running on automatic pilot, and the crewman on duty had only to watch the radar screen. He had been taught everything about the radar—except *what it was for*—and had gazed serenely as the blip indicating the island drew ever closer to the center of the screen, until finally the boat slammed head-on into the rocky shore.)

We had filmed sharks of several kinds, in situations both controlled and hairy: tiny Galápagos penguins (the northernmost penguins in the world), which swam like miniature rockets in pursuit of their prey; exotic critters like red-lipped batfish, which looked like a medical experiment gone awry, as if the body of a frog had been grafted onto the mouth of Carol Channing; seals and iguanas; Sally Lightfoot crabs and blue-footed boobies.

What we hadn't yet filmed were moray eels, which in the Galápagos (for reasons I know not) tend to congregate in large numbers in tight quarters. We had been told to expect to see four or five, or maybe more, eels poking out of a single hole, their heads jammed together, their jaws opening and closing as they respired in ragged synchrony. We hadn't seen it yet, but we kept looking, for we all knew it would make a wonderful image.

One day we found it—not once but several times—and it *was* wonderful and we filmed it till we ran out of film. Then, as we turned away, we noticed something curious: the eels were following us. We were on a rough, open lava plain, and from hidden holes all over the bottom, moray eels large and small, green and spotted, had come all the way out into the open and were chasing us.

Impossible. Morays *never* left the safety of their holes.

Oh, really?

We knew there was no point trying to flee; the morays could catch us up in a wink. And they did. And once they had us at their mercy, they . . . did nothing. They chased us, caught up with us, and passed us by.

It was frightening and—once we knew they didn't intend to bite us—fascinating and utterly inexplicable. None of us had ever seen anything like it before, and I haven't since.

Killer Whales (Orcas)

If there's an animal in the sea of which great white sharks have good reason to be afraid, it's the killer whale. Among meat eaters, it is *the* apex predator in the ocean. (Sperm whales, which are much bigger, are—technically—meat eaters, too, but their diet consists mostly of squid.) Though killer whales are officially members of the dolphin family, they make most dolphins seem like church mice. Males can grow to thirty feet long and weigh several tons.

Killer whales do eat mammals, and they have attacked and sunk boats—one celebrated incident was recounted in the book

Survive the Savage Sea—but there is *not one* recorded instance of an orca in the wild attacking a human being. There are, though, a couple of instances of captive killer whales turning on and wounding their trainers.

I was aware of all the facts and statistics when, in the 1980s, I was asked to go scuba diving in the wild with killer whales, but the knowledge was cold comfort: I didn't know anybody who had ever gone into the water with wild killer whales on purpose, so there was no one to call for advice. I thought that perhaps the reason nobody had ever been attacked was that nobody had ever been in the water with one. Maybe I'd be the index case, the first and foremost, the late, lucky loser.

The first protective measure I took was to have a wetsuit made, puke green with yellow piping on the arms and legs and a broad yellow stripe across the chest, designed to broadcast to any and all killer whales, *I am not a seal!* I considered having the actual words stenciled within the yellow stripe, but even I knew that, smart as they were, killer whales couldn't read English.

Killer whales exist in all the oceans of the world, in warm water and cold. According to Richard Ellis, they're the most widely distributed of all cetaceans (dolphins and whales). Their common name comes from the documented fact that they kill other whales. Pods of killer whales will gang up on one of the great whales—a blue whale, say—and kill it and eat it.

I was to dive with them in the cold Canadian waters of the Johnstone Strait, off Vancouver Island, where several pods were resident and being studied by scientists. Specifically, there was a particular stony beach where killer whales were known to come to rub themselves on the round rocks—called "rubbing rocks," in fact—either to rid themselves of minute parasites or, more likely, just for the fun of it. The plan was for Stan Waterman and me to lie on the rocky bottom, using oxygen rebreathers so as not to generate bubbles (whales hear them, know that they mean people, and stay away), and wait for the whales to arrive, at which point, with ABC's primitive video camera hard-wired to a monitor on the beach, we would capture images of them in an orgy of rubbing. (This has been done a thousand times since, but up till then it had never been done.)

I met my first killer whale before I even got wet. A local scientist and I were traveling across the Johnstone Strait in a rubber boat when we came upon a pod of orcas cruising easily in open water. We stopped the engine and drifted, and within five minutes the whales surrounded us, clicking and tweeping and chattering among themselves. There was a big male—easily identifiable by his five- or six-foot-high dorsal fin—along with a couple of females and a few youngsters.

Without warning, one of the youngsters—twelve or thirteen feet long and as big around as a barrel—surged out of the water and plopped its head on the side of the rubber boat. It opened its mouth, displaying its pink tongue and its huge conical teeth.

Shocked, I flinched and backed away.

"He wants you to scratch his tongue," the scientist said.

"Right," I replied, thinking that at this moment jokes were in rather bad taste.

"I'm serious. Go ahead."

I stared at him and at the whale, which was waiting patiently, mouth agape, emitting an occasional click or cheep. Then, having concluded that a one-armed writer could still be a writer, very gingerly I touched the whale's tongue and gave it a scratch.

"All the way back," the scientist said. "Right at the base. And really scratch it."

I took a deep breath and plunged my arm into the whale's mouth up to my shoulder. With my hand out of sight in the back of the dark cavern, I scratched for all I was worth.

The whale purred. I'm not kidding—it *purred*, just like a contented cat. And I—from the pit of my stomach to the back of my neck, where the hairs stood on end and tingled—felt overwhelmed by an almost celestial sense of awe, a conviction of communication not only with this young whale but with . . . I don't know . . . nature itself. I'd never experienced anything like it.

I looked at the scientist and grinned, and he grinned back. I scratched some more, the whale purred some more. I would've kept scratching all day, but after a while the scientist said, "That'll do," and I withdrew my arm. The whale closed its mouth and slid gently back into the sea.

The rest of our experiment with the killer whales of the Johnstone Strait was relatively uneventful. The water was wickedly cold, so we began by using dry suits, which, as the name implies, are intended to keep the diver dry and warm instead of, as in the case of a wetsuit, wet and clammy, but I have never gotten the hang of maneuvering inside what amounts to a gigantic space suit. I didn't know how to adjust my buoyancy; air pockets formed and shifted, so I hung askew, then shot to the surface upside down and backward. Forsaking warmth in favor of equilibrium, I switched back to my wetsuit, which allowed me ten or fifteen minutes of feeling in my hands and feet and approximately half an hour of consciousness.

The water over the rubbing rocks was only five or six feet deep but very murky (visibility between five and ten feet), and Stan and I lay on the bottom and waited for a pod of whales to come along for a rub.

We heard them long before we saw them; the clicks, whistles, and cheeps, I learned later, were the whales discussing *us*. Their supersensitive sonar picked us up from half a mile away, but they couldn't decide what we were. They knew we were alive and not fish, warm-blooded but not seals or sea lions. We exuded no bubbles. Evidently, we were worth investigating, for the whales continued toward us. Their conversation grew louder and more excited. (Stan and I later confessed that each of us had been convinced that the whales' discussion had been about which of them would have the privilege of deciding which of us to consume first.)

Louder and louder grew the whale sounds as closer and closer they came, and still we could see nothing but thick gray murk.

Suddenly, like a flash cut in a movie, the frame of our vision was filled with an enormous black-and-white head rushing at us. The jaws were agape; each cone of sharp white ivory shone like a blade.

And then the whale actually *saw* us, recognized us for what we were, and immediately—impossibly quickly—veered away, emitting a loud, long *blaaat*, the cetacean equivalent of a Bronx cheer, whose meaning (to me, at least) was vividly clear: disgust and dismay at being gulled by two dumb, clumsy, and decidedly inferior beings.

The immense body vanished; no other appeared, and as the pod pulled away from us, the tone of their discourse returned to a level of calm, desultory conversation.

Poisonous Animals

The oceans are full of creatures that depend on poison as a weapon of defense or offense. They range from anemones to corals to jellyfish, cone shells, bony fish, and air-breathing snakes.

Swimmers, in general, don't have to worry about any but the jellyfish, but there are so many kinds of jellyfish, with toxins of such a great variety of virulence, that it behooves a swimmer to seek the advice of locals before galloping willy-nilly into the water.

In Australia, for example, there are box jellyfish, called sea wasps, whose poison can, and occasionally does, kill a human being. At certain times of the year some beaches along Australia's northeast coast are closed to swimmers and surfers because of the seasonal invasion of sea wasps.

One of the most common dangerous jellyfish in the Atlantic is the Portuguese man-of-war, whose tentacles deliver a toxin that, while not usually fatal, causes excruciating pain and can be debilitating. The best thing that can be said about men-of-war is that you can see them coming: they are wind-and-current-driven jellies with "sails" like purple balloons that extend several inches above the surface. Visible though they may be, however, it's best to give them a wide berth; their stinging tentacles can extend as much as a hundred feet below and, depending on the current, to the side.

There are dozens of other stinging jellyfish that are more nuisance than menace, and almost all of them (including the sea wasps and the men-of-war) share a fascinating technology of attack. Their tentacles shoot microscopic harpoons, called nematocysts, into their victims, and the harpoons inject potent neurotoxins, or nerve poisons.

Humans are never any jellyfish's intended victim. A small fish stung to death by, say, a man-of-war is drawn up under the body— actually what Ellis calls "a colony of differentiated cells associated to form a functioning 'animal'"—and eaten with "feeding polyps."

There are almost as many proposed remedies for jellyfish stings as there are kinds of jellyfish—vinegar, urine, meat tenderizer, alcohol, seawater, and shampoo, to name a few—and many of them work, more or less, depending on the kind of jellyfish that has stung you, the amount of tentacle matter that has made contact with your skin, and the degree to which you are or aren't sensitive to the particular poison that has been injected. A woman I know swam face-on into one of the notorious "red jellies" that infest the Northeast every August, and she had to be hospitalized for a couple of days; at the same time a cousin of hers dove through a crowd of the same jellies and was stung all over her torso, and all she felt was an annoying tingling sensation—which may say as much about the highly subjective nature of pain as it does about jellyfish toxins.

Poisonous fish, many of which are of the family *Scorpaenidae* and include the scorpion fish, the lionfish, and the stonefish, are found in tropical waters and normally live near, on, or in the bottom, which is a blessing for swimmers and snorkelers because many of the family members are deadly. They have highly venomous spines on their backs, which are used entirely defensively, so no one need worry about being attacked by one. Stepping on one, however, is another concern altogether, and one that makes wading around reefs a perilous pastime.

Scuba divers worry about the *Scorpaenidae* for yet another reason: under water and within the kaleidoscopic chaos of color that is a tropical reef, they're almost invisible. Stonefish, which according to Ellis are the deadliest fish in the world, can look *exactly* like a rock covered with marine growth as they lie, half-hidden in the sand, and wait for potential prey to amble by. A wader who steps on one or a diver who reaches out to steady herself on this apparent rock may be stabbed by dorsal spines fed by venom glands. Untreated, an adult human can die in less than two hours.

Lionfish look like Christmas-tree ornaments designed by Hieronymus Bosch—gaudy, brazen, and armed with long venomous dorsal spines. They don't bother to hide, not in sand or reef, and they rarely retreat at the approach of a human. Instead, they'll seem to aim their spines your way, as if daring you to take your best shot. To me, the prime danger of a lionfish lies in its ability to disappear from view against the background of a particularly spectacular reef. Several times I've blundered up to and among lionfish without seeing them, and only good fortune has protected me from bumping or putting a hand on one.

I've had very little close contact with poisonous sea snakes, most of which live in the Indo-Pacific, and almost all of which want nothing whatever to do with human beings. There are several species; most are at least as venomous as the Indian cobra, but their fangs are very short and their temperaments usually placid. During breeding season, however, some species can become aggressive, and a couple of friends of mine have been surprised by snakes heading for the surface to breathe that suddenly reversed course, charged, and bit them. My friends' quarter-inch-thick wetsuits prevented the snakes' fangs from reaching their skin—or at least slowed the bite enough to give them time to grab the snakes and fling them away before fang touched flesh.

Barracudas

If ever there was a fish that's gotten a bad rap solely for being bad-looking, it's the barracuda. Up to six feet long, slender, tough, fast as lightning, and armed with a prognathous lower jaw (it extends forward beyond the upper one) studded with dozens of jagged, needle-sharp teeth designed specifically to tear prey to shreds, a barracuda looks to me like the Jack Palance of the sea: mean, menacing, and deadly. (I speak here specifically of the great barracuda, the largest of the more than twenty species that roam the tropical waters of the world.)

The image is a phony. While the great barracuda is capable, no question, of causing grievous bodily harm to any and all of us, it has no inclination to do so. It feeds on fish, and its speed and weaponry are so formidable that it has little difficulty catching and killing whatever it wants.

There have been very, very few cases of barracudas biting people, and all those I've heard of were, almost certainly, accidents of misidentification. A swimmer wears a shiny watch, ring, or buckle into the surf, where visibility is poor, and a barracuda mistakes a flash of reflected light for the shimmer of fish scales. It bites, instantly recognizes its error, and vanishes. Sometimes the bite is so fast and efficient that the person doesn't know he's been bitten.

Divers are accustomed to seeing barracudas appear from nowhere, as if by teleportation, hang around and gaze with fixed eye at whatever's going on, and then disappear with the same impossible speed. Sometimes they come very close and hover, motionless, watching; usually, they establish and somehow maintain a precise distance from the divers, advancing and retreating without appearing to flutter a single fin.

I have never heard of a barracuda seeing a human being, watching, studying, and appraising him, and then turning on him and biting him. Never.

Which was no comfort at all when one day I took Wendy and then-twelve-year-old Clayton drift diving off Palm Beach, Florida.

Drift diving is diving in—and with—a strong current, and it is done in circumstances where swimming against the current is difficult, dangerous, or downright impossible. Divers leave the boat in one location, drift along with the current—holding a line tethered to an inflated ball that bobs on the surface so the captain of the boat can keep track of them—and are retrieved by the boat far down-current when the dive is done.

Palm Beach is perfect for drift diving because one of the world's great currents, the Gulf Stream, effectively touches the shore right there as it sweeps north, and eventually northeast, warming the Atlantic waters all the way from Bermuda to Newfoundland and points east. Dive boats can deposit divers only a couple of hundred yards offshore, where instantly they're seized by the warm, four-knot current and carried along with the entire movable feast that inhabits the Gulf Stream.

Four of us jumped into the choppy water—we three and a dive master, who held the line tied to the floating ball—and quickly sank to the calm and quiet thirty or forty feet down. The water was so rich in nutrients that it was cloudy; visibility was terrible, and Wendy and I made sure to keep our eyes on both Clayton and the dive master.

There wasn't much to see, however, and Clayton soon became impatient. Not content with the speed with which we were roaring along, he increased his velocity by kicking with the current.

Within thirty seconds he had vanished into the gloom.

Though Wendy and I were both concerned, we weren't particularly worried: he couldn't stray too far, and he could only stray in one direction because he couldn't possibly swim against the current.

Then there he was, suddenly, chugging directly at us, against the current, kicking as fast as his fins would flutter, breast-stroking with his arms, staring at us through the faceplate of his mask, his eyes wide with fear. Implausibly, he was making headway, and when he reached us he kept swimming until he was behind me, and then he stopped struggling, grabbed me, and climbed aboard my back.

I looked at Wendy, who was looking at Clayton, who was pointing somewhere ahead as, in exhaustion, he breathed so fast that bubbles exploded from his regulator in a constant stream.

We looked, following his finger, but saw nothing. I was beginning to assume that Clayton had inadvertently come up behind, and perhaps startled, a shark that had turned toward him, scaring him out of his wits, when I saw Wendy pointing and then the dive master pointing, and there, a few yards ahead and below, was what looked like a big school of big sharks, just cruising along in the current, as if waiting for food to be carried to them.

But they weren't sharks. As we drifted closer and closer, and they slowly rose to meet us until we were actually drifting *among* them, I saw that they were barracudas, and not merely great barracudas, for the word *great* doesn't do them justice. They were super-, mega-, Moby barracudas, barracudas on steroids.

I couldn't believe it. Even allowing for the fact that, under water, everything looks a third again as big as it really is, these monsters couldn't be real. They were at *least* twelve feet long. Which meant that they were really nine feet long.

Nine-foot barracudas! They were two feet high and one foot thick, and each one's mouth looked like a Swiss army knife open for display. Their eyes stared at us with the blank serenity of the invulnerable.

It took me several minutes to rein in my mental hyperbole. As we continued to drift together, and these great creatures paid us no attention whatever—they moved aside, in fact, to avoid contact with us—I could finally see them in proper perspective.

There were probably a dozen of them—it was hard to tell, for they drifted in and out of sight—and each one was probably five or six feet long and very high and very thick. As I gazed at each silver giant, I now saw, instead of ugliness, the beauty of perfection, for in their world these creatures were supreme. They went where they wanted, ate what they chose, and feared no living thing.

When at last we surfaced and were back on the boat, Clayton said, "I think I'd like to be a barracuda."

Rays

The oceans are full of rays of all kinds, colors, shapes, and sizes. All are "cousins" of the sharks, in that they're technically elasmobranchs; their bodies are structured not with bones but with cartilage. They include everything from sawfishes to guitarfishes to manta rays, eagle rays, and stingrays, and—except for the most bizarre of accidental circumstances—they're harmless to humans.

But what about stingrays? I hear you yowling. *They have stingers, don't they? They can sting you, can't they?*

Yes, they can, if you step on them. But so can bees. And a bald eagle can claw your eyes out, and a German shepherd can rip your throat out, and a raccoon can give you rabies. But the chances are, they won't.

Anyone who needs convincing of the general benevolence of stingrays need travel no farther than the Cayman Islands, where local dive groups have established a dive site called Stingray City, in the sand flats off Grand Cayman. Stingrays gather there in numbers far too large to count, and they wait patiently for the boats that arrive daily with divers and food. The rays swim up to you, under your arms, between your legs, around your head; they envelop you with wings as soft as satin; they feed from your hand, and if you have nothing for them, they move on to someone else. (Even stingrays can make mistakes, however: a few years ago, one mistook my son-in-law's wrist for a tender morsel, and actually bit him. The hard cartilaginous plates in the ray's mouth caused a nasty bruise but didn't break the skin.)

It's very tempting to anthropomorphize stingrays, because not only do they behave calmly and comfortably around humans but, when seen from underneath, they can even *look* humanoid, if you'll let your imagination ramble a bit. The nostrils look like eyes, the mouth is a mouth, and the point of the head can become a nose, and . . . well, you have to be there. Ellis points out that long, long ago, stingrays dead, dried, and doctored were known as "Jenny Hanivers" and were displayed as proof of the existence of mermaids.

Twenty years ago I had an experience with a ray that changed my life. Literally. Not only did I hurry home and write a book about it—*The Girl of the Sea of Cortez*—but it altered forever my perception of animals, people, the sea, and the interconnectedness of everything on earth.

I was in the Sea of Cortez, doing an *American Sportsman* segment on hammerhead sharks, which for reasons no one has ever been able to ascertain gather there periodically in huge, peaceful schools of hundreds, perhaps thousands, at a time. The gatherings seem to have nothing to do with either breeding or feeding; the hammerheads are simply there, in crowds so thick that, seen from below, they block the sun.

The underwater cameramen on the shoot were old friends, Stan Waterman and Howard Hall; Howard's wife, Michele, who's now a producer, director, and partner in Howard's film company, was along in the dual capacities of nurse and still photographer.

One afternoon, when we returned to our chartered boat, the *Don Jose,* full of macho tales of death-defying diving among the anthropophagi, we were interrupted by a very excited Michele, who directed us to look beneath the boat.

There, basking in the boat's cool shadow, was the largest manta ray any of us had ever seen. (We'd soon learn that it measured eighteen feet from wing tip to wing tip; for the moment, all we knew was that it looked as big as an F-16.) Its unique cephalic fins, which would unfurl during feeding and become supple sweeps to gather food into the immense maw, were rolled up tightly now, and they looked exactly like horns—thus, the manta's age-old traditional name, devilfish.

For centuries the manta was one of the most terrifying animals in the sea: huge, horned, winged, with a mouth big enough to swallow a person whole and a proclivity for leaping clear out of the water, turning somersaults, and *slamming* down upon the surface of the sea, obviously daring any foolish sailor to fall overboard into its ghastly grasp. Equally obviously, such hideous monsters deserved no fate better than death, and spearing mantas used to be a popular sport among the few, the bold, and the brave.

In fact, mantas are harmless. They eat only plankton and other microscopic sea life. They breach (soar out of the water) for reasons no one knows for certain, probably to rid themselves of parasites but possibly, as I prefer to believe, just for the hell of it. Usually, they avoid people, swimming—*flying* seems more accurate—slowly away from approaching divers.

Sometimes, however, they seem to seek the company of people; witness the manta that now rested peacefully beneath our boat. Before any of us could ask, Michele told us how she had discovered the magnificent creature.

The air temperature was well above a hundred degrees Fahrenheit. The *Don Jose* was not air-conditioned. To keep bearably cool, Michele went overboard frequently, and on one of her plunges she had seen the enormous ray hovering motionless beneath the boat. She swam toward it. It didn't move. As she drew near, she saw that the animal was injured: where one wing joined the body there was a tear in the flesh, and the wound was full of rope. Michele supposed that the manta had swum blindly into one of the countless nets set by fishermen all over the Sea of Cortez. In struggling to free itself, which it had accomplished not with teeth (they have none) but with sheer strength, it had torn its wing and carried pieces of the broken net away with it.

Michele kept expecting the manta to ease away from her as she approached, but by now she was virtually on top of it and still it hadn't moved. She was, however, out of breath; she decided to return to the boat and put on scuba gear.

The manta was still there when she returned. This time she was emitting noisy streams of bubbles, and she *knew* that the manta would flee from them.

It didn't.

Slowly, she let herself fall gently down until she was sitting on the manta's back.

Still it didn't move.

Michele reached forward and, very gingerly, pulled strand after strand of thick rope netting out of the ragged wound. She had no idea how—or even if—rays experience pain, but if they did, she thought, this *had* to hurt.

The manta lay perfectly still.

When all the rope was gone, Michele carefully packed the shreds of torn flesh together and pressed them into the cavity in the wing. She covered the wound with her hands.

Now the manta came to life. Very slowly it raised its wings and brought them down again, and very slowly the great body began to move forward, not with enough velocity to throw Michele off its back but with an easy, casual pace that let her ride comfortably along. To steady herself Michele put one hand on the manta's six-foot-wide upper lip, and off they went, with Michele's heart pounding in her chest, elation filling her heart, amazement and delight flooding her mind.

The boat was anchored on a sea mount, an underwater mountain whose peak extended to within a hundred feet of the surface, and with unimaginable grace the manta took Michele on a flying tour of the entire mountaintop. Down it flew to the edge of darkness, then up again to the surface light.

Michele didn't know how long the ride lasted—fifteen minutes, maybe half an hour—but eventually the manta returned to its station in the shadow of the boat and stopped. Michele let go and came to the surface: incredulous, thrilled beyond words, and knowing full well that we would never believe her because surely, by the time we returned, the manta would have long since returned to its home range, wherever that might be.

But it hadn't. It was still there, still resting in the cool, still apparently—impossibly!—willing to have more contact with humans.

We decided to try to capture the manta on film. We knew we couldn't duplicate Michele's experience, but even if we could get some shots of the great ray flying away, with a human being in the same frame to give a sense of its size, we'd have some very special film.

When Howard and Stan had filmed the ray itself from every possible angle, they signaled for me to descend, as Michele had, and attempt to land gently on the manta's back. I had done my best to neutralize my buoyancy so that, once submerged, my 180 pounds would weigh nothing, and now I used my hands like little fins to guide me down upon the animal as lightly as a butterfly.

As soon as the manta felt my presence on its back, it started forward. It flew very slowly at first, but soon its wings fell into a long, graceful sweep, and it accelerated to a speed at which I—in order to stay aboard—had to grip its upper lip with one hand and a wing with the other and lie flat against its back. My mask was mashed against my face, we were going so fast, and my hair was plastered back so hard that on film I look bald.

I felt like a fighter pilot—no, not a pilot, for I had no control over this craft; rather, like a passenger in a fighter plane. Down we flew, and banked around the sea mount, and soared again. We passed turtles that didn't give us a passing glance and hammerheads that (I swear) did a double take as they saw us go by.

The world grew dark, and for a moment I was afraid—I knew we had gone very deep, but I had no way of knowing exactly *how* deep because I couldn't let go with one hand to retrieve my depth gauge. *If we're too deep,* I worried, *I'll run out of air, or get the bends on surfacing, or—*

Just then, as if to reassure me, the manta returned to the world of light. It rushed for the surface, gaining speed with every thrust of its mighty wings, and I had the sudden, terrifying conviction that it was going to burst through the surface and take to the air—and me with it—and when we slammed down again on the water I would be reduced to pudding. But long before it reached the surface, the manta swerved away and began to cruise twenty or thirty feet below the boat.

Finally, it slowed, then silently stopped directly in the shadow of the boat. I let go and made my way to the surface.

Like Michele, I didn't know how long my journey had lasted, and there was no way to find out. My air tank was almost empty, and Stan and Howard had each run through a full load of film, which meant that I had been under water on that magical ride for at least twenty minutes. But how deep, and for how long, at what depth? The only way I would know how much residual nitrogen remained in my system—the villain that brings on bends—was to wait. If I came down with the agony of the bends, in my joints or my guts, I'd know I had gone too deep for too long. If I didn't, I'd know I hadn't. Simple as that.

The manta, meanwhile, remained beneath the boat. Over the next three days, every member of the crew had a chance to swim with or ride on the manta, and always, without exception, the wonderful ray returned its passengers to the same exact spot beneath the boat.

As soon as I returned home, I began to write, for a story had been born, entire, in my head. I wrote it at record speed (for me) and with thoughts, feelings, and perceptions I didn't know I had.

It was published as the novel *The Girl of the Sea of Cortez*, and though it's now out of print, I'm delighted that readers (especially young ones) are still discovering it, for it is my favorite of all my books about the sea.

Though the book still clings to life, I'm sorry to report that the magical manta rays of the Sea of Cortez do not. Too many fishermen lost too many nets to the mantas, and so they hunted them down and killed them.

Squid—Giant and Otherwise

Of all the creatures that have ever lived in the sea, none, I warrant, has generated more groundless fears and fabulous fantasies than the giant squid. Jules Verne had a giant squid attack the submarine *Nautilus* in 20,000 *Leagues Under the Sea*. I wrote a novel about a giant squid, titled *Beast,* which NBC made into a miniseries. And Richard Ellis, who knows more than I ever will about giant squid, published a fine, comprehensive, and accessible nonfiction book called *The Search for the Giant Squid.*

Ellis's title is particularly appropriate, for almost the entire history of man's relationship with this most formidable of all invertebrates has been a search, and a fruitless one at that. One of the main reasons—if not *the* main reason—for our endless fascination with this monster of monsters is that so very, very little is known about it. And the reason for *that* is that despite twenty-first-century technology and vast expenditures of money and time by battalions of intrepid scientists and adventurers, no one has ever seen a giant squid alive in its habitat—that is, the ocean. What fragments are known have been gathered from studies of specimens either dead or dying in the nets that have ensnared them.

Here, in a combination of facts from Ellis's encyclopedia and my own experiences, conversations, and reading, is a distillation of what's known about giant squid.

Their scientific name is *Architeuthis,* which translates from the Greek (roughly) as "first among squids," not first in line but first in importance, as in "squid of all squids" or, in today's parlance, "Man, you de *squiiiid.*" There are more than a dozen different species of *Architeuthis,* most named for the place their corpses were found, but amateurs like me bundle them all together with the single name *Architeuthis dux:* king of kings of squids. Sort of.

They are the largest of the more than seven hundred kinds of squid that live in the world's oceans. The biggest one accepted by science—the dead animal, found decades ago washed up on a New Zealand shore, was complete—was definitively measured at fifty-seven feet long, from its tail to the tip of its two "whips," or feeding tentacles. (Unlike octopuses, squid have *ten* arms, eight short ones plus the two whips.)

The biggest one accepted by *me* was seventy-three feet long; by the time it washed up on a beach in eastern Canada, some of its arms had been eaten away, so it could not be accurately measured, but reputable scientists extrapolated from the substantial remains that the animal would have been seventy-three feet long.

I'm prepared to believe, furthermore, that somewhere in the deep ocean there lives a giant squid more than a hundred feet long. While I was doing research for *Beast* more than a decade ago, I spoke by phone with one of the world's two great teuthologists (squid scientists). He was ill then and would die soon thereafter, and though he was helpful and forthcoming, he insisted that I not attribute anything he said directly to him, for he didn't want to risk his reputation or his place in the pantheon of teuthology. He told me that his lifetime of study had convinced him that the existence of a *150-foot* giant squid was not only possible but probable.

Imagine a squid half the length of a football field . . . a squid that, standing on end, would reach fifteen stories into the air . . . a squid longer than three locomotives . . . a squid . . . well, you get the idea.

Giant squid seem to inhabit the oceans' midwater range, between 1,800 and 3,500 feet; that, at least, is where most of the specimens caught recently in fishing nets have been found. There is practically no light at those depths except for what is generated by creatures that are themselves bioluminescent (like many squid), and giant squid have enormous eyes (the largest in the animal kingdom) that can attain a diameter of fifteen inches and, presumably, can gather in every available atom of light.

Throughout history (all the way back to Homer) there have been stories of giant squid attacking and sinking ships. Many of these tales have been supported by witnesses and newspaper accounts, but none have been completely authenticated. Countless stories exist of monster squid assaulting fishermen and plucking hapless shipwreck survivors from lifeboats. None of those would stand up in court, either, though I'm convinced that several, though perhaps wildly exaggerated, spring from seeds of truth. There are, simply, too many accounts by too many rational people with too little to gain by fashioning silly fictions for them *all* to be fantasies or hallucinations.

Certainly, giant squid have the equipment with which to wreak havoc on small boats and all humans. Although *Architeuthis* does not have (as I posited in *Beast*) claws within each sucker on its tentacles—claws that are present in many smaller, more aggressive species of squid—its suckers *do* possess rings of hard, sharp "teeth" made of chitin (the same stuff some mollusk shells are made of), which gnaw into prey and drag it toward the animal's big, sharp beak. The beak, in turn, slashes the prey to pieces and feeds it to the squid's studded tongue, which forces the flesh down into the gut.

A lovely way to go, no?

Among the many things *not* known about giant squid are how big they can grow, how fast they grow, how long they live, exactly what they feed on (it *is* known that sperm whales feed on *them*), where they hang out, whether or not they are aggressive, whether or not they are as immensely powerful as legend insists, and why they die. Every year, all over the world, a great many giant squid just seem to die. Because their flesh is loaded with ammonium ions, which are lighter than water, their bodies float rather than sink. Some are consumed by sharks and other fish, but some float all the way to shore more or less intact.

My fascination with giant squid began in the late 1970s, when Teddy Tucker and I decided to try to catch one off Bermuda, where giant-squid bodies—and pieces of bodies—were found floating on the surface quite often. We went out at night and from the stern of his boat lowered two 3,000-foot lengths of cable woven of forty-eight strands of stainless steel. Each cable carried clusters of baited hooks of varying sizes, plus Cyalume chemical lights, which, we hoped, would attract the squids' attention.

We had visions of grotesque monsters in the Stygian deep, throbbing with the colors of excitement (all squid have in their flesh chromatophores that allow them to change color with the speed of a strobe) as they attacked our baits; of titanic struggles as the cables thrummed with strain and spat droplets of water from each stressed strand; of the stern of the boat being pulled down, down, until—perhaps—Teddy would decide that the only way to save our lives would be to sever the cables with the axe he had stowed by the transom.

We waited all night, bouncing around in rough seas, and got nary a nibble on either cable. At dawn, morose with disappointment, we began to haul in the cables on giant spools.

They came in easily. Too easily, in fact. *Strange.*

The five-hundred-foot marker passed, then the thousand-foot, and with every turn of the spool the cable seemed lighter, much lighter, weirdly light. The fifteen-hundred-foot marker passed, and now the cables felt *too* light. Definitely.

Over the stern the cables popped. The lights were gone, the baits were gone, the hooks were gone. The final thousand feet of cable were gone.

The cables had been severed. They hadn't popped from weight or stress; the strands were all still tightly wrapped. They had been cut. Bitten off.

Gloom gave way to excitement. What could have done this? Not a shark; no gigantic fish had swallowed the baited hooks and tried to run with them. We would have felt it; the boat would have moved. And no shark tooth was hard enough to cut through an eighth of an inch of stainless steel.

We couldn't have foul-hooked a whale. Sure, the weight of a whale would have been enough to break the cable, but the cable ends would be splayed, the strands all askew.

Whatever had bitten through our cables, we decided, had a beak as hard as Kevlar. (How, you ask, could we make that leap of logic? Easy: we wanted to.) And what had such a beak?

Why, nothing—nothing, that is, except a giant squid.

Clearly, this was an animal worth pursuing.

We tried the next year, and the next. We've tried, in fact, every year since then. Always we've been teased; never have we been successful.

We've hung cameras down to two and three thousand feet and focused them on baited hooks. We've seen creatures bizarre and wonderful—vicious little squid that savaged our bait till all that was left were scales; curious, unknown sharks that live only in that particular part of the deep—but never a sign of *Architeuthis*.

One day we set a baited line half a mile down and buoyed it with three rubber balls, each designed to float five hundred pounds. We left the line for a couple of hours while we went to set others, and when we returned, the balls were gone.

For fifteen or twenty minutes we searched back and forth. There was no question that we were in the right place; Teddy has an uncanny ability to locate himself in the open ocean, especially off Bermuda, where he can pinpoint his position by triangulating landmarks.

The balls were gone. Simple as that.

Just as we were about to abandon them—yet another mystery never to be solved—there was a roaring, whooshing sound off the port side of Teddy's boat, and one by one—*Pow! Pow! Pow!*—the three balls burst through the surface, still connected together, and bobbed placidly on the calm sea, as if they'd never been gone at all.

When we pulled in the half mile of line—heavy-duty polypropylene rope, to be precise—all the hooks were gone, as were all the baits, and, once again, the strands of the rope were still tightly bound. Something had pulled and pulled and pulled, with a force great enough to sink three quarters of a ton, and then bitten through the rope.

In the early 1990s, when I was host of an ESPN series of shows called *Expedition Earth,* produced by the enterprising and indefatigable John Wilcox, we spent nearly three years putting together an hour on giant squid. Because we knew that the chances of our being able to film one in the wild were close to nil, we filmed some of the animals closely associated with *Architeuthis.*

We traveled again to Canada, this time to dive—in January, no less, and in falling snow—with the squid's fabulous cousin, the giant octopus. Documented as large as sixteen feet in diameter, but averred in legend to grow to greater than twenty feet from tentacle tip to tentacle tip, giant octopuses are shy, reclusive, and, when they can be coaxed out of their dens, fascinating to watch as they scurry across the sea floor, changing color and pattern to camouflage themselves to match the bottom they're on or over.

We swam with Caribbean sperm whales in the deep waters around Dominica and Martinique, hoping—against all odds—to catch some interaction between whale and squid. The only squid I saw, however, were ex-squid, former squid, squid that (like the famous Monty Python parrot) were no more; as I snorkeled beside a fifty-foot-long adult sperm whale, she sounded, and left me, as a parting gift, enveloped in a thick red cloud of eaten, digested, and excreted giant squid.

We acquired old woodcut prints of beached giant squid, amateur video footage of giant squid killed in fishing nets, and some extraordinary footage shot by Howard Hall of a hundred-pound Humboldt squid—considered by Mexican fishermen to be more dangerous to man than any sharks—ripping apart a big tuna being hand-fed to it by Bob Cranston. (One of Howard's other colleagues was later attacked by three Humboldt squid and was lucky to escape with his life.)

In the end we put together a good hourlong show that was, I believe, informative and entertaining—all, of course, without once succeeding in finding a single giant squid.

Over the past decade, more and more dead and dying giant squid have been caught by net fishermen, particularly in the waters off New Zealand. The reason is not a sudden population increase in giant squid but relatively recent technological advances that have given deep-sea trawlers access to fish in water two thousand to five thousand feet deep. There, evidently, the squid spend a good deal of their time feeding on, among other things, a species of midwater fish called orange roughy.

Orange roughies are amazing fish, only about a foot long, that can live for more than a century. Ellis says that "there are documented records of individuals that have reached 150." They don't mature until they're about thirty years old, and because they tend to gather in tight schools, they're easy prey for deep trawlers. A five-minute trawl, according to Ellis, "can fill a trawl net with 10 to 50 tons of fish."

Consequently, orange roughies are being wiped out at an alarming rate. The fishery is only twenty-three years old, and already catches have declined drastically. Some scientists believe that orange roughies may eventually set a record for the speed with which any species (of anything) has gone from initial discovery to commercial extinction.

Meanwhile, though, the presence of giant squid among the orange-roughy populations has lured legions of passionate teuthophiles (squid lovers)—scientists, writers, divers, and filmmakers—to embark upon multimillion-dollar expeditions to find giant squid by using submersibles, fifty-thousand-dollar-a-day ships, and the highest of high-tech locating gear.

None has ever seen a giant squid—let alone caught one or filmed a live one swimming in the sea—and, I confess, I'm glad.

Architeuthis is one of the few true mysteries left on earth, an animal of mythic stature that we know exists but we cannot find, a real creature that is at the same time an ancient, enduring legend, a spur to scientific quest and an inspiration to mankind's imagination.

It is the last dragon. We need our dragons, for they help our fancies soar beyond the boundaries of grim reality.

I hope that the giant squid successfully eludes us for years to come, for to find the dragon will be to kill it, and to make it disappear forever.

14

Even *More* Creatures
to Avoid . . . and Respect

AMONG THE IMMENSE CITIZENRY OF THE SEA THERE ARE IN-
numerable other living things that appear to be immobile, inert,
innocuous, inanimate, or sentient and even friendly . . . but that
can, in fact, be dangerous to the uninitiated, the careless, or the
unlucky.

Many **corals** are poisonous to the touch; they possess stinging
cells that are used both for defense and to paralyze prey. The most
common of the toxic corals—at least as far as swimmers, snorkelers, and divers are concerned—is fire coral, which looks like mus-
tard that has been painted onto parts of a reef. Slick, motionless,
and innocuous-looking, fire coral can deliver a thoroughly nasty
sting to an inquiring hand.

Sea anemones are poisonous, too. Their beautiful, waving
tentacles present themselves as harmless because colorful little

fishes swim all around them with no ill effects. In fact, each ten-tacle is armed with nematocysts that fire toxic harpoons into any-thing that touches them—except the colorful little fishes (usually clownfish), which are coated with a mucus that renders them im-mune to the anemone's poison. The relationship is pure symbio-sis: the anemone protects the clownfish from other predators; in return, the clownfish removes food particles and other debris from the anemone, keeping it clean and healthy.

Several species of **mantis shrimp** can grow to more than a foot in length, including those that live in the North Atlantic, the Mediterranean, and Australia, where they're known as "killer prawns." If that sounds melodramatic, consider: each has a pair of limbs that fold like the forearms of a praying mantis (hence the name). The limbs *un*fold like a jackknife, at the speed of light, and the blades are so strong and sharp that they can amputate a human finger with a single stroke. Mantis shrimp are fearless and aggressive, and I know several underwater photographers who are seriously afraid of them; when a photographer is concentrating on getting a macro shot of an infinitesimal creature hiding in a reef, he isn't thinking about what might be burrowed in the sand beside him, ready to pounce and slash his flesh to ribbons.

Spiny sea urchins, black, bristly balls that live on the sea bot-tom, are harmless—until you happen to step on or bump into one, at which point one or more of the hundreds of spines spear you and break off in your flesh. Some species have poisonous spines and some don't, but *any* urchin spine is amazingly painful, difficult to extract (they keep breaking apart into smaller and smaller pieces), and a potential infection.

Some oceangoing critters are obviously dangerous and to be

avoided at all costs: **saltwater crocodiles** leap quickly to mind. Years ago, during one of my futile attempts to translate Roger Caras's book *Dangerous to Man* to television, I worked with a researcher from the National Geographic Society to assemble a list of the ten most dangerous animals in the world. We found it impossible not to include saltwater crocodiles.

They live all over the western Pacific, in freshwater rivers and brackish swamps as well as in the sea. They eat virtually anything they can catch, and they stalk and catch almost anything: birds, monkeys, turtles, fish, crabs, buffaloes, and—documented many times—human beings. They're known to grow to at least twenty-three feet long (Ellis says they're the largest of all the living reptiles), and they regularly swim hundreds of miles out into the open ocean.

A friend of mine was once contemplating a trip around the Pacific in a collapsible kayak, and one part of his journey would take him across the Torres Strait, which separates northern Australia from New Guinea. He asked me about the chances of his encountering aggressive sharks. I told him I wouldn't be half so afraid of sharks as of the "salties," which have been known to attack and destroy boats much more substantial than collapsible kayaks.

A version of the saltwater crocodile lives in the mangrove swamps around Cuba (and, I assume, elsewhere in the Caribbean), but it is much smaller. I believe that it's technically a caiman, which means it's a closer relative to an alligator than a crocodile. David Doubilet was introduced to one while we were doing a story on underwater Cuba, and he found it to be quite docile.

Still . . .

Other sea creatures have completely surprised me when, over the years, I've discovered in them a dangerous trait. But in every case I've come to realize that it's the human that has gotten in harm's way, not the animal that's suddenly turned mean.

I'm speaking here specifically of **groupers**, **bluefish**, and, believe it or not, certain species of **dolphins**.

The one dicey moment I've witnessed with a grouper happened in the Turks and Caicos Islands, a small archipelago south of the Bahamas. A woman in our crew had decided to go for a swim during the heat of the day, and she dove off the boat without giving a thought to the fact that she was in a very active phase of her menstrual cycle. She was wearing a two-piece bathing suit, the bottom half of which was brief but not scandalously so.

She had been in the water for perhaps twenty or thirty seconds—she had surfaced from her dive and wiped her hair back from her face—when she felt something bump her, very hard, in the thigh, and then bite her.

She shouted and lashed out with her feet, trying to back away. She wore neither mask nor fins, so she couldn't see what had bitten her, nor could she escape with any speed. It pursued her, bit her again, and kept coming. Again she shouted.

Those of us on board heard her shout, ran to the side, and looked overboard. Through the gin-clear water we could see everything: a small (eight- or ten-pound) Nassau grouper had, we assumed, scented blood in the water and, following its instinct, attacked the source. Never mind that the animal it was attacking was more than ten times its size: that animal was bleeding, and blood meant injury, weakness, and vulnerability.

It took us a few seconds to realize that what we were watching was not funny. Then two of us jumped overboard, one right behind the swimmer, one right on top of the grouper, which—startled to find that the sky had fallen on its head—shot away to the safety of the reef below.

We escorted the woman to the back of the boat, helped her up onto the dive step at the stern, and were astonished at the damage wrought by the small, young, normally placid fish: the inside of one of her thighs had been torn, and blood was flowing from ruptured veins. Fortunately, the fish had not bitten deep enough to slash through the femoral artery, which could have caused serious, even mortal, damage.

In January 2002 a report came in from Australia about two divers being harassed by a *six-foot-long,* several-hundred-pound grouper that seemed intent on trying, at least, to eat them. It sneaked up on one diver and took his entire head in its mouth. Only quick, aggressive action by his buddy saved the diver from serious injury, or worse.

I grew up knowing how violent and voracious bluefish could be during a feeding frenzy. Every summer I fished for them off Nantucket, and when birds were working on a school of baitfish and bluefish were attacking from below, the carnage was mesmerizing. The blues would roll and leap and dive, snapping at everything with their scalpel-sharp, triangular teeth, and often we'd decide not to bother throwing a lure into the mêlée because there'd be no sport to it: a bite was all but guaranteed in writing.

From the safety of the boat, I never gave a thought to what would happen to a person who found himself in the water amid an orgy of feeding bluefish.

A lifeguard in Florida found out. He was sitting on a surfboard in calm water less than a hundred yards offshore when, first, flocks of gulls and terns drove a huge mass of baitfish toward him, and then he saw—he could tell from the sudden, roiling chop in the glass-calm sea and the glint of sunlight off the scales of rolling fish—that a school of blues was assaulting the baitfish.

He watched, spellbound, as the feeding frenzy came closer. He didn't move, didn't paddle away, just sat there with his feet dangling over the sides of the surfboard.

So fast did the bluefish strike and so sharp were their teeth that two of the lifeguard's toes were gone before he could yank his feet out of the water.

In the newspaper account I read, the lifeguard didn't talk about the pain he felt, or what he had done to stem the flow of blood from his mangled foot while he paddled ashore. All he would discuss, all that seemed to be on his mind, was the terror he felt at the prospect of a dozen frenzied bluefish flinging themselves onto his surfboard and continuing to chomp on him, and the ultimate horror of what would happen if, through panic or clumsiness, he capsized his surfboard, fell into the water, and was eaten to death by a thousand ravenous fish.

Nature has spent millennia creating balanced ecosystems all over the world: on one island, just the right kind and number of snakes to keep the bird and rodent populations in check; on another, the proper plants to nourish the resident animals, and the appropriate insects to pollinate the plants.

On huge, isolated landmasses such as Australia, which contain several disparate kinds of environments—jungles, deserts, mountains, forests, and coastlines that vary from straight and sandy to cold and rocky to warm and swampy—disparate natural balances have evolved. Animals, plants, and insects live well together, feed and sustain one another, and maintain viable populations with one another.

The sudden introduction of **new species**—almost always by humans, intentionally or not—can, and usually does, disrupt those natural balances. Sometimes the disruptions are catastrophic to local populations. In the Galápagos Islands, for example, the introduction long ago of pigs and goats (from passing ships) destroyed populations of birds and reptiles that laid their eggs in the ground. And nowadays, tourist cruise boats inadvertently transport colonies of insects from one island to another, creating chaos among resident plant and insect populations that have no defenses against the newcomers.

Some of the Hawaiian Islands have lost almost all their native birds to an invasion of voracious snakes from Guam that, scientists believe, have hitchhiked their way across the Pacific in ships' cargoes and sometimes in the wheel wells of passenger jetliners.

The so-called "killer bees" from Africa were brought over to South America by scientists trying to create a productive new strain of bees. Inevitably, some of the bees escaped, and over the past several years they have gradually made their way north up the American continent, overpowering and crossbreeding with native species and creating ferociously aggressive new strains of ill-tempered bees.

Kudzu was imported into the American South, where, because it has no natural predators, it has overrun enormous areas of several states. Gypsy moths were imported into the American North by a well-meaning but wrongheaded scientist, and they've become a plague upon our trees.

Another instance of man attempting to manipulate nature put me and my family into one of the weirdest encounters of my life.

Wendy, Christopher, and I were in Moorea, the island forty minutes by fast boat across the Sea of the Moon from Tahiti. Christopher was ten, and this was the second year we had taken him with us to explore the waters of Polynesia while I did a story for a magazine. He was already an accomplished diver, and over the next couple of years he would become more so as he accompanied us on two voyages to explore the underwater world of the Galápagos.

Our hotel in Moorea featured a swim-with-the-dolphins attraction. I'm aware of the controversy surrounding human contact with captive marine animals, especially captive cetacea (dolphins and whales), and, with a few specific exceptions, I'm against holding large cetacea in captivity.

Still, we decided to try this program. Christopher had never been in the water with a dolphin, and besides, the facility in Moorea was not a normal captive-interaction program. It seemed to me to be particularly enlightened: for one thing, the two trained dolphins were not captives—they had access to the open ocean, were free to come and go as they pleased, and had been conditioned only to return to the tank at the hotel twice each day, when they would be fed and permitted—the trainer swore that they didn't have to be coaxed—to interact with a few humans.

Before we entered the tank, the trainer explained to us that the two dolphins were of an especially intelligent branch of the family *Delphinidae:* rough-toothed dolphins, a male and a female, approximately eight feet long. They were not trained to do tricks; they would simply come to us when and as they chose and swim among us, and though we could extend our hands and feel the hard, slick skin as the dolphins passed, we were not to grab a dorsal fin and hitch a ride or to try to hold or impede the dolphins in any way.

The tank was approximately four feet deep and a hundred feet in diameter, and when we were all in the water, the trainer signaled to his assistant, who opened the gate between the tank and an exterior holding pen.

Immediately the two dolphins swam into the tank. For a moment they paused together on the far side, like (I imagined) two vaudeville performers facing a small audience and discussing how best to wow them. And then . . . well, first I'd better explain something:

At the moment when what happened was happening, I hadn't a clue as to what was really going on, or why. Not until several days later, after conversations with people who knew a great deal more about dolphins than I do, did I understand how and why a macho-mad dolphin had threatened my life.

When the trainer told us that rough-toothed dolphins were smarter than most, he neglected to add that they're also temperamental and difficult. Other dolphin experts used words such as "cranky," "aggressive," and "darn well dangerous."

While the male and female paused on the opposite side of the tank from where we were, they were studying us. Literally. Using their phenomenal sonar, they scanned our bodies, inside and out, and were able to determine our genders, our ages, and our positions in the sexual strata of mammals. Here's what they perceived: our party consisted of one presexual male (Christopher), one sexually active female (Wendy), and one sexually active male (me). To the male dolphin, Christopher was no threat, Wendy was a potential possession, and I was—very definitely—a potential rival for its position as alpha male. I was to be dispensed with, one way or another.

The dolphin's great intelligence was, at once, the cause of my peril and my salvation. If its brain had been smaller, more primitive and less developed, it wouldn't have had the impulse or the ability to perform such a detailed analysis of humans in its presence; nor, however, would it have had the supersophistication to choose between issuing a warning and launching an outright attack.

Why, I will never know—perhaps it took pity on me as a schlemiel—but it decided to warn me, not kill me.

All I did know was that, from a dead stop, in what seemed like a fraction of a second, the bigger of the two dolphins had crossed the tank, passed between Christopher and Wendy without touching either, and—with a final, powerful thrust of its broad tail (which did wallop Wendy and leave her with a permanent dent in the thigh)—rammed me, at full speed, precisely between my legs.

It knew exactly what it was doing, what it was aiming to hit and what it was aiming to miss. It didn't want to injure, maim, or kill me, or surely it would have and certainly it could have. (Dolphins can and do butt sharks to death frequently, and once in a great while they kill humans who tease or otherwise mess with them.) It wanted to warn me. It was saying, This is *my* turf, bub, and all females herein are mine, so *scram!*

The four- or five-hundred-pound dolphin was too big to pass between my legs, so when it struck me it lifted me high into the air, out of the water, and thrust me several feet away. I recall a weird sensation of having been hit by a torpedo, so hard and slick was its skin.

In a wink the dolphin zipped away, circled, and started back again, to—well, I'll never know—but the trainer, who had watched the assault dumbstruck, came to life, blew his whistle, waved his hands at the dolphin, and stepped between the dolphin and me.

The dolphin stopped so suddenly that it would have left rubber, had it had wheels.

"Get out!" the trainer shouted to us, over his shoulder. "Get out of the pool!"

We three waded to the edge of the tank and hoisted ourselves out of the water. Only then did Wendy feel the pain in her leg and see the deep, purple crease in her thigh.

Christopher hadn't understood any of what had just transpired, and he was laughing himself silly. He thought the dolphin had been playing.

I? I felt confused and slightly sick.

The trainer covered his embarrassment and surprise by sending the dolphin away with angry hand signals. This was an aberration, he told us; nothing like it had ever happened before. Ever, ever, ever. He promised. And it would never happen again. He would teach the dolphin a lesson by punishing it: it wouldn't be allowed to play with any more humans for the rest of the day.

He said he hoped that I wouldn't feel compelled to mention the incident in the story I was writing, for—truly—never in all his years, et cetera.

I said I saw no reason to publicize the episode. After all, no one had been seriously hurt, and this *was* a fluke.

The next day David Doubilet, who had been taking pictures on another island, arrived on Moorea and, without contacting us, visited the same "dolphinarium."

The same dolphin did the same thing to him, driving him from the tank before he could snap a single picture.

As tempting as it was to lay all the blame on the operators of the facility, I knew that, really, I had only myself to blame. I hadn't been savvy enough about the particular species of dolphin, and I had violated one of the fundamental precepts of venturing into the sea, by making my wife and young child vulnerable to the instincts and urges of a large, strong, and—above all—*wild* oceanic predator.

So eager can we be to humanize all the world's animals that we forget to respect the most precious element in an animal's life: its wildness.

Finally, there's the peril that cruise-ship operators, tour organizers, and dive-group leaders don't like to talk about: **piracy**. Over the last decade or so, piracy has become one of the fastest-growing, serious, life-threatening, no-kidding dangers to scuba divers and sailors all over the world.

Boats and ships of all sizes are being seized, their cargoes plundered, the vessels themselves repainted and renamed or abandoned or sunk, and their passengers and crew frequently murdered. Dive resorts on remote islands are being invaded and the guests killed or taken hostage, sometimes in the name of one or another radical religion, sometimes in the name only of greed.

Drug pirates, of course, have been a plague on the Caribbean and the southern North Atlantic for years, with criminals often seeking "clean" boats with legal registrations in which to ferry their cargoes ashore in U.S. ports. In the early 1980s Teddy Tucker and I and our crew were set upon twice by drug pirates who swooped down on us in small speedboats and retreated only when we brandished an arsenal of assault rifles. (Nowadays, we wouldn't stand a chance: some pirates are armed with bazookas, grenade launchers, and heavy machine guns.)

According to the International Chamber of Commerce's Commercial Crime Services, 469 attacks by pirates were reported in the year 2000. Seventy-two people were killed—six times the number reported killed by shark attacks—and another hundred were injured.

Of the attacks, 119 took place in Indonesia, 75 in the waters between Malaysia and Sumatra, and 55 off Bangladesh. The rest were scattered all over the planet. The vessels assaulted ranged from huge bulk carriers to mom-and-pop sailboats.

Everywhere the numbers were up from the year before.

Those figures represent only the attacks that were *reported*. They don't take into account the boats and people that merely went missing, as if, in a single gulp, they were swallowed by the sea.

15

Okay, So What Can *We* Do?

ON A BEAUTIFUL AUTUMN DAY IN LATE MARCH 1999, I KNELT inside the belly cavity of a gargantuan great white shark and helped a scientist hunt for its heart.

In life, she had been nearly eighteen feet long—longer than all but the biggest sport-utility vehicles—and had weighed nearly two tons. By now, after a year of being frozen, she had shrunk by a foot and had lost a few hundred pounds of water weight.

Still, the two of us fit easily within her, and when the *National Geographic* cameraman approached for a close-up, there was ample room for him as well.

This leviathan had died, or been killed, or had killed herself— the difference between interpretations was not insignificant and depended on your attitude toward animals and nature and mankind's relationship to both—by rolling up in a coastal longline set to catch big Australian snappers, becoming ensnared, and finally asphyxiating. Like all sharks of her kind, she stayed alive only by constantly moving forward and flushing oxygen-rich water over her gills. Once immobilized, she died of anoxia—lack of oxygen.

The fisherman who found her had towed her to shore and notified the authorities. Though it was illegal to kill a great white shark in the state of South Australia, this death had obviously been accidental, and no charges were lodged. In fact, the police expressed their gratitude to the fisherman; he could easily have cut the shark away from his line and let it sink to the bottom. When he asked for permission to keep the jaw, however, his request was denied: a great-white-shark jaw this huge might fetch ten thousand Australian dollars from a collector, and news of such a sale might encourage other fishermen to discover other "accidental" catches.

The scientific community expressed its collective regret that the enormous predator had died, but individual scientists were delighted to have the opportunity—very rare, indeed—to study a fully mature, intact, and undamaged female great white shark.

First, though, they had to find a freezer large enough to hold her until they could decide exactly what to do with her and how and where to do it. They located a gigantic cold box a few miles outside Adelaide, and there they stowed this special specimen— until now.

I had been working for months on a story for *National Geographic* magazine and a television special for NGTV about great white sharks, to be published (and broadcast) in the spring of 2000, as close as possible to the twenty-fifth anniversary of the release of the movie version of *Jaws*. David Doubilet and I had proposed the story as a vehicle through which to gather photographs the likes of which had never before been taken (his responsibility) and to assemble all the new information about great whites that had accumulated in the quarter-century since the film had burst upon the public consciousness (mine).

When John Bredar, the gentle, genteel, and gifted producer/ director of the television film, told me that the gigantic shark was about to be brought in from the cold, thawed, and studied, I quickly volunteered to return to the other side of the planet, where we had been diving with great whites only a couple of months earlier.

Thawing the shark took several days—well, hey, do *you* have a microwave capable of defrosting a thirty-five-hundred-pound fish?—and on the first day she was displayed, on a trailer bed at the South Australia Research and Development Institute (SARDI) outside the town of Glenelg, twelve thousand people waited in line for hours, in a driving rain, for the chance to see, touch, feel, and smell the most formidable predator any of them had ever seen—or, probably, ever imagined.

She was magnificent even in death. Her length, her breadth, her sheer bulk struck spectators dumb. Her inch-and-a-half-long upper teeth were irresistible to wide-eyed children, who ran their fingers over the serrated sides of each white triangle and thought thoughts that would surely return to them in the dark of night. Nobody said much, and those who did speak kept their voices low. I heard not one smart-mouth crack, not one lame joke, and I knew that if someone had uttered even a mild expression of cynicism, the crowd would have turned on him and shamed him into silence.

The folks were fascinated, yes, and awed, but as the hours

passed and the crowd kept shuffling through, the sentiment I felt permeating the atmosphere most thoroughly was reverence. What they were seeing was not merely a legend come true, but tangible evidence of the power of elemental nature. For several people this was, I was certain, a moment of epiphany.

The next day the shark was moved farther out of town, to the Bolivar Maceration Facility, a big, hangarlike building on open land beside a sewage-treatment plant, where whales and other large marine animals that washed up onshore were cut to pieces and rendered into disposable constituent parts.

Bolivar was where Dr. Barry Bruce, an eminent SARDI biologist from Tasmania, and I would be filmed dissecting the great white shark. (Actually, of course, he would dissect and comment while I watched and asked questions.)

Bolivar stank. Oh, my, did it stink! Every square inch of every surface, every atom of air that flowed from and around the great gleaming tanks full of putrefying flesh reeked with a nauseating pungency that brought tears to our eyes. (Though I was given a chic yellow rubber apron to wear, along with striking black rubber boots and lovely pink rubber gloves, the stink invaded and so completely inhabited every fiber of my cotton clothes that eventually, after a few futile launderings, I would be forced to wrap them in plastic and put them out with the garbage.)

The shark lay on her back, tilted slightly to port by the protrusion of her rigid dorsal fin, which shifted her massive insides leftward in a bulge that threatened to roll her off the dissecting table. Barry and his team of assistants and students had placed buckets and plastic vats all around the table, to catch whatever fell out when the shark was opened up. While Barry honed the twelve-inch blade of a carving knife, John Bredar placed me, his cameraman, his lights, and his sound equipment in positions perfect to announce and record any and all discoveries.

Nobody knew what we would find inside the shark, and nobody speculated aloud about the possibilities, though we all silently shared the same thoughts. *A keg of nails? Half a horse? A whole swordfish? A sea lion? A human leg? An entire person?* All of these and a thousand other implausible objects had been found before inside great white sharks.

Barry placed the point of his knife against the belly of the beast; I cleared my throat; the cameraman said the magic word, *speed,* telling John that the camera was rolling at the proper rate; John gave Barry a quiet "Action!" and the dissection began.

Have you ever daydreamed about plunging your knife into the belly of a marauding shark? Perhaps you're diving down to open the treasure chest or rescue the fair maiden when suddenly a dark shadow falls over you and the giant shark attacks. You duck below the monster, reach up with your knife hand, and slide the blade into the soft white flesh of the underbelly, splitting it open like a ripe melon and sending the mortally wounded shark off to die in the deep.

Well, forget it. Your knife would either bounce off or break off, and you'd face a future as lunch.

While Barry labored to slice through skin—no, *meat!*—more than an inch thick, he explained that female great whites are armored by nature to protect them during mating, which is a violent affair punctuated by repeated bites from the male desperate to maintain his grip on the female. "Remember," Barry said, "they don't have hands, and they have to hold on *some*how."

As the slit in the shark's belly grew longer, pressure increased from within, and cutting became quicker.

Someone said, Watch out.

For what? I asked.

The liver. It's a third of the body weight. Here it comes!

And here, forcing its way out through the hole in the shark, came a thousand-pound liver, the immense organ of energy storage that permitted the shark to go without eating for a month or more after one substantial meal.

For a couple of hours the dissection proceeded methodically. Barry described each of his findings, first in layman's terms for the camera, then in scientific jargon for the tape recorder monitored by one of his aides.

The shark's fins were sliced off, and as each was tossed into a bin, we spoke of the sorry fact that there were people all over the world who would gladly have butchered this shark for her fins alone.

Though she bore old mating scars on her flanks, and though her uterus was stretched (indicating that she had borne young), she was not pregnant when she died.

We took breaks—to change tapes and batteries and to rinse our lungs with fresh air—and during one I was taken on a hunt for specimens of Australia's notorious endemic funnel web spider. Small (about the size of your thumbnail) and inoffensive-looking, Australian funnel webs are among the most poisonous spiders on the planet and, unfortunately, are common in populated areas like suburbs. It took us less than five minutes to find several—in a woodpile, under discarded equipment, beside a corner of the building—which reinforced my conviction that Australians are some of humanity's hardiest and most sensible people.

Wherever they live, travel, hike, swim, fish, dive, kayak, or trek, they risk being confronted by *some*thing capable of doing them in with tooth, fang, claw, jaw, or stinger, and yet there is no public clamor to eradicate any animal because of the peril it poses to the human population. Australians have learned to coexist in relative peace with nearly everything, and when occasionally a human life is lost to an animal, the public usually reacts philosophically.

It was after noon when Barry determined that the time had come to open the shark's stomach and examine its contents. What would be in there? We all watched with childlike anticipation.

Barry slit the stomach sac, and following an initial deluge of liquid, there came . . .

. . . not much, really, except confirmation of how the shark had died. The stomach contained three intact fifteen- or twenty-pound snappers, swallowed whole and complete with hooks, leaders, and lengths of line, and a few bits and pieces of other prey: beaks from small squids and octopuses, otoliths (bony pieces from the inner ear) from different fish, which would be studied later, and a four-inch-long stingray barb whose owner must have been consumed a long time ago, for it had already migrated through several inches of dense flesh on its way to rejection by the shark's amazingly rugged defense mechanisms.

We shared a feeling of anticlimax: inside the shark there were no billfish, seals, or walruses, whole or in part, no priests, scientists, or politicians—not even a license plate or two.

By now, our excitement had been replaced by subdued silence, for as Barry reached up behind the jaw and felt around for the shark's heart, we could see that the once magnificent creature had been reduced to little more than a memory. Only the head remained intact, and even that now radiated not power but pathos.

What I felt most, I think, was sorrow at the waste. The death of this giant had benefitted no one. Maybe Barry and his team would come up with discoveries or conclusions that might help protect other sharks; maybe the children in the crowds that had stood in line to see the great white would grow up with respect and affection for the animals. I hoped so, because otherwise the net result of this accidental catch and all the attention and effort attending it would be merely one less apex predator in the critical food chain at the bottom of the world.

Nature is very careful with her apex predators. They were not made with man in mind—remember, they've been present on earth, more or less exactly as they are today, for scores of millions of years—and they cannot survive interference, accidental or intentional, from humans.

At the rate at which great whites are being killed all over the world, the existence of certain populations is already threatened, and the survival of the entire species may soon be in doubt.

Our grandchildren may be able to know great white sharks only from film and videotape.

The same is true, to a greater or lesser degree, of other sharks and other fish.

Ideologues of every stripe, as well as folks with interests economic, political, or personal, can interpret data and statistics to suit their own purposes, but a few unalterable facts resist interpretation: every major fishery in the world is being overexploited, pushed beyond its capacities. At a time when a swelling human population needs more animal protein than ever, catches of almost every important food fish are in decline.

Everywhere, too many fishermen with too much sophisticated gear are chasing too few fish.

In retrospect, the shark-attack hysteria of the summer of 2001 seems to have been a diversion. Yes, an unfortunate youngster whose case lit the fuse was attacked by a shark. Yes, others, too, were attacked, and four died. Those were tragic accidents that can't be denied, mustn't be diminished, and won't be forgotten. But they were neither unprecedented nor inexplicable.

The sensational "summer of the shark" was a creation of the media, and only in that regard was it extraordinary. Seldom in recent centuries have so many spent so much energy, print, and airtime trying to discover and deftly explain the cause of something that hadn't happened, wasn't happening, and didn't exist.

We mustn't let ourselves be distracted from the genuine problems that do exist in the sea, problems that can be solved only by us and only if we will reexamine our place in nature and rethink our conduct as members of the natural order.

My personal guide are some words written by the naturalist Henry Beston in his 1928 classic, *The Outermost House,* and I end with them because additional words would be superfluous:

> We need another and a wiser and perhaps a more mystical concept of animals. Remote from universal nature, and living by complicated artifice, man in civilization surveys the creature through the glass of his knowledge and sees thereby a feather magnified and the whole image in distortion. We patronize them for their incompleteness, for their tragic fate of having taken form so far below ourselves. And therein we err, and greatly err. For the animal shall not be measured by man. In a world older and more complete than

ours they move finished and complete, gifted with extensions of the senses we have lost or never attained, living by voices we shall never hear. They are not brethren, they are not underlings; they are other nations, caught with ourselves in the net of life and time, fellow prisoners of the splendour and travail of the earth.

ABOUT THE TYPE

This book was set in Fairfield, the first typeface from the hand of the distinguished American artist and engraver Rudolph Ruzicka (1883–1978). Ruzicka was born in Bohemia and came to America in 1894. He set up his own shop, devoted to wood engraving and printing, in New York in 1913 after a varied career working as a wood engraver, in photoengraving and banknote printing plants, and as an art director and freelance artist. He designed and illustrated many books, and was the creator of a considerable list of individual prints—wood engravings, line engravings on copper, and aquatints.